Intellectual Property Rights and Copyrights

S.P. Satarkar

M.Sc., M.Lib.Sc., Ph.D.

University Librarian

Swami Ramanand Teerth

Marathwada University, Vishnupuri, Nanded

Ess Ess Publications

4837/24, Ansari Road, Darya Ganj,

New Delhi-110002

☏ : 3260807, 3201533

Fax : 3274173

E-mail: essess@del3.vsnl.net.in

url:http://www.essessbooks.com

First Published 2003

ISBN : 81-7000-350-4

Price : Rs. 600

Published by:

Ess Ess Publications

4837/24, Ansari Road, Darya Ganj,
New Delhi - 110 002
Phone : 3260807
Fax : 3274173
E-mail : essess@del3.vsnl.net.in
url: http://www.essessbooks.com

Laser Typesetting:

Mukesh Graphics

L-2/8, DDA Market
Mangolepuri, New Delhi
Ph. : 7924405

Printed at :

Print Line

Contents

SECTION-3 : Violation of Copyrights and Librarianship

SECTION-4 : Intellectual Property Rights International Scene

LIST OF CONTRIBUTORS

Barad, P.H. Assistant Librarian, Anuradha Engineering College, Anuradha Nagar, Sakegaon Road, Chikhli, Dist.Buldhana-443 201.

Das, B.B. Reader, P.G.Department of Law, Berhampur University, Bhanja Bihar, Berhampur- 760 007.

Deshpande (Dr.), Neela, Librarian, Jaykar Library, University of Pune,Ganeshkhind, Pune

Dominic, J, Assistant Librarian,Karunya Institute of Technology,Karunya Nagar Post,Coimbatore-641 114.

Ganpule (Dr.) S.R. 9/142, Kannamwar Nagar,Vikhroli, Mumbai-400 083.

Goel (Ms) Sridevi, IPS, Spl.IGP and Chief Security & Vigilance Officer,Maharashtra. State Road Transport Corporation, Maharashtra Vahatuk Bhavan,Dr.Anandrao Nair Marg,Mumbai- 400 008.

Gupta, V. K. Scientist, National Institute of Science Technology & Development Studies (NISTADS), Dr.K.S.Krishnan Marg, New Delhi.

Gyananath (Dr.) G. Reader, School of Life Science Swami Ramanand Teerth Marathwada University,'Dnyanteerth' Vishnupuri, Nanded-431 606.

Gokhale, (Dr.) Mrs. P. A. Department of Library & Information Science, University of Mumbai, Jawaharlal Nehru Library, Vidyanagari, Santacruz (East), Mumbai- 400 098.

Joshi, J.V. Head School of Commerce and Management, Swami Ramanand Teerth Marathwada University, 'Dnyanteerth' Vishnupuri, Nanded-431 606.

Karmarkar, (Dr.) P. G. 3/13/A, Shivam Complex, Rajaji Path, Ram Nagar, Dombivali (East)- 421 201.

Kokate, R. G. Librarian Anuradha Engineering College, Anuradha Nagar, Sakegaon Road, Chikhli, Dist.Buldhana-443 201.

Kuffalikar, (Ms.) Chitra Rekha 28/512 Narayan Niwas, Rashmi Apartments, Landra Park, Old Ramdaspeth, Nagpur-440010.

Kulkarni , J.N. Assistant Librarian Swami Ramanand Teerth Marathwada University, 'Dnyanteerth' Vishnupuri, Nanded-431 606.

Kumar, (Dr.) P.S.G. Dr.V.B.Alias Bhausaheb Kolte Library, North Ambazari Road, Nagpur-440 010.

Nirmala P.J. Assistant Librarian,Karunya Institute of Technology,Karunya Nagar Post,Coimbatore-641 114.

Naidu , (Prof.)M.K.R. Ashish Co-operative Housing Society, 4, Bunglow, Andheri (West), Mumbai.

Prasad (Dr.) K.V. Director, Institute of Information Studies, 702, Upstairs, 42nd Cross, III Block,Rajajinagar, Bangalore-560 010.

Panda (Dr.) Bhavani Prasad Reader, P.G.Department of Law, Berhampur University, Bhanja Bihar, Berhampur- 760 007.

Panda, (Ms) Minati Advocate, Berhampur 760007

Rajhansa (Ms.) Vijaya Prof. & Head,Dept. of Library & Information Science, University Librarian, Jawaharlal Nehru Library, Vidyanagari, Santacruz (East), Mumbai- 400 098.

Raju, (Prof.) A.A.N. 3-10-63, Gokhale Nagar, Ramanthpur, Hyderabad-500 013.

Riswadkar, M. R. 389/1, Shaniwar Peth, Pune – 411 030.

Satarkar (Dr.) S. P. University Librarian, Swami Ramanand Teerth Marathwada University, 'Dnyanteerth' Vishnupuri, Nanded-431 606.

PREFACE

Intellectual Property Rights hold importance in almost all walks of life, be it the field of agriculture, biotechnology and also in library & information science. Copyrights are mainly concerned with authors, publishers, librarians, persons related to film industry and music industry. Patents, trademarks, information sources, movies, gramophone records, cassettes and computer softwares are directly related to intellectural products. Persons from revenue, police, law and judiciary are actively engaged in protecting these rights. With the new inventions in science and technology, there is rapid growth in production of the equipments useful for duplicating or copying. This has resulted in malpractices, which affect the Intellectual Property Rights of the owners. In true sense, the Intellectual Property Rights & Copyrights cover not only printed matter but the patents, industrial designs, trademarks, trade secrets, layout designing of integrated circuits and so on. Librarians are deeply concerned with these rights as their work is closely related to the acquisition, storage and retrieval of information.

Only preparation of laws for protection of Intellectual Property Rights does not fulfill the aim. Execution of the laws effectively and awareness of these laws among the society play an important role in its success. Such awareness can be effectively created by the educational institutions.

The intellectual Property Rights and Copyrights are important not only at national but also at international level. The two international conventions on copyright namely the Berne Convention for the Protection of Literary and Artistic Works (1948 Brussels Text) and the Universal Copyright Convention (1952) have played an important role in creating the atmosphere useful to protect the copyrights at international level. These conventions were revised at Paris in 1971. This revision which provided certain additional facilities to enable the developing countries to grant compulsory licenses for translation and reproduction, and works of foreign origin required for the purpose of teaching, scholorship or research or for purposes of systematic instructional activities. India being a member of these two international conventions has amended the copyright act of 1983 in which further amendments were made in 1984 and in 1992.

We are facing many challenges in the field of Intellectual Property Rights. Different countries have claimed the patents related to the agricultural products. Considering the globalization and GAAT, considerable thought and deliberations have attempted to evolve a consenses on trade related Intellectual Property Rights. These have also been adopted by World Trade Organization. Various laws in order to preserve biodiversity and to safeguard our agricultural products were passed by the Parliament of India. However, due to the increased number of researches carried out in the universities and in other research institutions, it has became essential to create such environment in which there will not be a malpractice or piracy of original products.

Intellectul Property Rights and Copyrights ensure the originaters such a protection so that even a new design, logo, trademark can be protected for its misuse. Even a piece of art, literature, computer programme, biological wealth or cultural heritage can be protected with the help of these acts. However, the people are not adequately aware about the Intellectual Property Rights and Copyrights. The present volume discusses all these issues in depth and I hope it will present the scenario properly.

The volume is divided into four sections. First section stresses need and importance of Intellectual Property Rights and Copyrights, second section deals with Intellectual Property Rights & information technology. Third section discusses violation of copyrights and librarianship. Fourth section describes Intellectual Property Rights at international level. The papers included in this volume have considered the impact of Intellectual Property Rights on agriculture biotechnology, music industry, copyrights and cybernetics. The contributors of the papers include 12 librarians, 4 teachers of library science, 2 scientists, 2 judges, 1 teacher of law and 1 police officer.

Because of the diversity of these professioners, the volume provides calidioscopic view of IPR & copyrights. The authors of these papers are not only from Maharashtra but also from Andhra Pradesh, Karnataka, Tamilnadu, Delhi etc.

The book will be useful to the librarians, scientists, educationists and the persons working in revenue, law, judiciary and police departments and even for a common man. However its success remains in the fact that how effectively the IPR & Copyrights are protected in our day to day life, by a common man.

Editor

ACKNOWLEDGEMENTS

Present volume is an outcome of the seminar on "Intellectual Property Rights and Copyright Matters" held at Swami Ramnand Teerth Marathwada University, Nanded, Maharashtra on 8th & 9th February 2002. The seminar was sponsored and financially supported by Ministry of Human Resource Development, Government of India, New Delhi and was organized by the university library.

22 papers were presented in the seminar and are included in this volume. The seminar took place in four sessions. The first session has emphasized the need and importance of the Intellectual Property Rights and Copyright; in which eight papers were presented. Impact of information technology on Intellectual Property Rights was emphasized in second session; in which five papers were presented. Third session was about violation of copyrights and librarianship, which was discussed through five papers. Fourth and last session was about international scene and Intellectual Property Rights; which was explained by five papers.

Eminent personalities like Mrs. Sridevi Goel, Inspector General of Police, Mumbai; V.K.Gupta, Scientist, National Institute of Science, Technology and Development Studies, New Delhi; M.K.R.Naidu, Professor emeritus in Library and Information Science Dr. S. R. Ganpule, former Librarian, Indian Institute of Technology, Mumbai and many others have participated in the seminar.

The seminar was inaugurated by Hon. Shivraj Patil Chakurkar, Member of Parliament and former Speaker of Loksabha and was concluded by Dr.T.A.V.Murthy, Director, INFLIBNET, Ahmedabad. Hon. Justice S.G. Mutalik, former High Court Judge was present as a Chief Guest throughout the deliberations.

I am thankful to Dr. S. A. Suryawanshi, Vice Chancellor. Swami Ramanand Teerth Marathwada University, Nanded whose encouragements resulted in the successful organization of the seminar. We are grateful to Hon. Shivraj Patil Chakurkar, Hon. Justice S.G.

Mutalik, Dr. T.A.V. Murthy for gracing the occasion and for their valuable guidance.

As an editor of the volume, I express sincere thanks to the authors of the papers whose contribution to this volume is invaluable.

I also, express thanks to my colleagues Shri. J. N. Kulkarni, Shri. R.G. Dharmapurikar, Shri R.D. Kale and Shri. G. K. Hambarde who actively participated in preparation of this volume.

Last but of most importance is the support extended by Ministry of Human Resource Development, New Delhi, without which it would not have been possible to achieve the venture. I am deeply indebted by its support.

I am thankful to M/s Ess Ess Publications, New Delhi for accepting the volume for publication.

"Dnyanteerth", Vishnupuri

Nanded

Dt. 24.07.2002

Editor

Section 1

IPR and Copyright : Need and Importance

1

INTELLECTUAL PROPERTY RIGHTS AND COPYRIGHTS: CHALLENGES OF COMMING DECADE

M.K.R. Naidu

In recent times issues related to Intellectual Property Rights (IPR) have been debated in various conferences and forums in India. The rapidly changing scenario and India's continuing progress towards economic upliftment and globalization through liberalized policy make it imperative that the potential beneficiaries of the IPR system familiarize themselves with basic elements of IPR to maximizes their exploitation. However we notice that IPR does not find a rightful place in our education system and its importance is not realised. This neglect has resulted in our scientists, researchers and innovators of ideas proper appreciation of the basic concepts of IPR and their utilization. The role played by patents, copyrights, etc. has been comparatively less or negligent. No less than a person, the great scientist, Dr. R.A. Mashelkar, the Director General, C.S.I.R. New Delhi in his article recently published in Journal of Chartered Secretary (January2002) felt that "Twenty first century will be the century of knowledge, indeed the century of the mind. Innovation is the key for the production as well as processing of knowledge. A nation's ability to convert knowledge into wealth and social good through the process of innovation, will determine its future. In this context, issues like generation, valuation, protection and exploitation of intellectual property (IP) are going to become critically important all around the world. Exponential growth of scientific knowledge, increasing demands for new forms of intellectual property protection as well as access to IP related information, increasing dominance of the new knowledge economy over the old brick and mortar economy, complexities linked to IP in traditional knowledge, community knowledge and animate objects, will pose a challenge in setting the new 21st century IP agenda.

An ideal regime of intellectual property rights strikes a balance between private incentives for innovators and the public interest of maximizing access to the fruits of innovation. This balance is reflected in Article 27 of the 1948 Universal Declaration of Human Rights, which recognizes both that "Everyone has the right to the protection of the moral and material interest resulting from any scientific, literacy or artistic production of which he is the author" and that "Everyone has the right.... To share in scientific advancement and its benefits." The burning question seems to be balancing the interest of the inventor and that of the society in an optimum way.

New ideas and inventions, which keep on emerging in every conceivable field of science and technology, are the outcome of manipulation of human mental faculty. The resulting outcome of human intelligence is known as 'intellectual property'. It is therefore, essential to protect such intellectual property so that nobody else can enjoy the fruits of other's efforts. There are several ways to protect this intellectual property. Patent rights can protect inventions. A new design, similarly, can be safe-kept by properly registering it. New logos and labels as trademark, on the other hand, can also be protected as registered trademarks. A piece of art, literature, cinematographic film, musical record and computer programmes can be registered for their legal protection under copyright law. Biological wealth and cultural heritage can be protected under geographical indications by properly documenting them.

It is essential that in the interest of the individual, country and society at large scientific inventions, new technologies and creative achievements be protected so that the respective innovators, designers and other professionals can gain rewards, which they deserve. There has been a growing realization that with the rapid progress of information technology, evolution of global media and communication revolution, there has been phenomenal increase in copying, counterfeiting and similar other malpractices and owners of intellectual property are severely affected by such piracies. Patent and copyright laws differ widely between nations, which affect trade and investment flow between nations and also give rise to trade and industrial disputes. The various national and international efforts in this direction could not do much to alleviate the problem. The Uruguay Round of GATT negotiations which concluded in December, 1993 after considerable thought and deliberations has attempted to evolve a consensus on Trade Related Intellectual Property Rights (TRIPs) which has been adopted by World Trade Organisation (WTO).

Intellectual Property Rights can be defined as the rights given to persons over the creations of their minds. They usually give the creator an exclusive legal right over the use of his/her creation for a certain period of time and thus protect the owner against unauthorised copying or imitation.

As per TRIP (Trade Related Intellectual Property Rights), the types of IRPs are i) Patents, ii) Copyrights and related rights, iii) Geographical indications, iv) Industrial designs, v) Trademarks, vi) Layout designs of integrated circuits, and vii) Trade secrets (undisclosed information). Further, amongst the different types of TRIPs the legal dimensions concerning the patent particularly and geographical indications to some extent involve the whole lot of discussions.

The social purpose is to provide for the results of investment in the development of new technology, thus giving the incentive and means to finance research and development activities.

A functioning intellectual property regime should also facilitate the transfer of technology in the form of foreign direct investment, joint ventures and licensing.

The protection is usually given for a finite time (typically 20 years in the case of patents).

It should also be noted that the exclusive rights given are generally subject to a number of limitations and exceptions, aimed at fine-tuning the balance that has to be found between the legitimate interests of right holders and of users.

Historically property rights in knowledge; information or reputation is a capitalist innovation. The practice was started in the Italian City states, first formalized in a Venetian law of 1474. The practice spread to other countries of Western Europe. In the reign of Elizabeth I, a series of patents to encourage foreign inventors to import their inventions and work them in England and also to help domestic producers were made. However, the Statue of Monopolies of 1674 placed a number of restrictions to create monopolies. England passed a series of laws for patents for the benefit of its inventors. The Act of 1852 consolidated a number of patents given. The British Government in 1856 enacted a similar law (Act on Protection of Inventions) in India. It was modified in 1859. Later the Patents and Designs Protection Act of 1872, followed by Protection of Inventions Act in 1883 and Inventions and Designs Act in 1888. After independence we had Indian Patents and Designs Act, 1947. A major change occurred with the passing of Patents Act (Act 39 of 1970) which came into force in 1972. Later further changes were made in 1990s.

Copyright

As per Common Law, copyright is defined as the right to prevent publication. Statutes have extended the definition to include the right to prevent others from multiplying copies. Copyright is now defined as 'the sole right in the case of unpublished works to produce or reproduce any literary, dramatic or musical work or any substantial part of a work in any material form whatsoever, provided the author is qualified to hold copyright'. (As per Encyclopedic Dictionary of Library & Information Science).

Copyright includes the sole right to produce, reproduce, perform or publish any translation of a particular work, to convert a dramatic work into a novel or non-dramatic work, to convert a novel or other non-dramatic work or any artistic work into a dramatic work, to make any record, film, sound or television broadcast or any other contrivance for performing or delivering any literary, dramatic, or musical work, and to authorize any of the above acts.

There can be no copyright in an idea. Copyright exists only when that idea is published in any form of words or form of expression such as a play or picture.

Copyright normally expires after a period of 50 years from the end of the calendar year in which the author dies. Performances which include delivery of lectures, addresses, speeches, surmons and other means of visual and acoustic presentation, artistic works, engravings, photographs, works of architecture, artistic craftsmanship are for a period of 50 years after the author's death. Generally ownership of the copyright lies with the author. However if he is employed or in the service of the employer, the copyright lies with the employer who has commissioned the work. The owner of the copyright may assign his rights wholly or partially, generally or limited to an area, for the whole remaining period or part provided he does so in writing signed by the owner or his authorized agent. Licenses may be granted on payment of a fee for performance or reproduction on limited occasions. A copyright thus helps a copyright holder with a kind of monopoly over the created material. This assures him of both control over its use and economic benefits derived from it.

Historically, copyright grew out of the same system as royal patent brands, which gave the authors and the printers the exclusive rights to publish books and other materials. The purpose was too providing government to increase its revenue and control over publication content. This system was in use by the Italian city states namely Venice. Later England, France and other western countries adopted this. The Statue of Anne passed in 1710 was a milestone in the history of copyright law. It was important as it recognised that the author should be the primary beneficiary of the copyright law. It also established the idea that such laws should have a limited duration after which such was cook pass into public domain. It established duration of 28 years after the work is published. Many other states in western world enacted similar laws. With the development of technology in the communications there was concern over the protection of author's rights on an international scale. France extended the protection of its copyright laws regardless of nationality. Thus began a moment of international agreement, which finally came at a meeting held, what is popularly known as Berne Convention of 1886. Originally USA opposed Berne Convention, Later it agreed to the Berne Convention in 1998. Its Act of 1978 authorised Congress to create a national copyright system to promote the progress of Science and Arts for a limited time to authors – the exclusive right to their writings. By the Semiconductor Chip Protection Act of 1984, the USA extended protection for mask works fixed in a semiconductor chip product. Under certain conditions computer programs may receive patent protection where the program is a product or process claims. The copyright royalty tribunal was established with the power to adjust the royalty rates and to redistribute the royalty fees. The Act of 1978 also laid down copyright protection as the life of author plus 50 years. The Second International Convention was held in Geneva in 1952. The Universal Copyright Convention (UCC) provides for same protection of foreign works as for domestic works. It also provides exclusive rights for translation upto 7 years.

Indian scenario as regards Intellectual Property Rights is characterised by extreme illiteracy as regards patent system, copyright and other issues included under TRIPs. We have not been able to adopt common agreed conditions. A number of our author's, designers, artists have suffered monetary loss for non-enforcement of these legal rights. The classic case is of R. K. Narayan who preferred to get his works printed abroad rather than in India. Our people also do not take their patent rights seriously and timely. The cases of Turmeric, Neem, Basmati etc, which are mostly Indian products but got patented abroad, are some of the examples of our laziness and non-realisation of our rights. It is very important that our people should be educated and be provided with all facilities to realize their rights of IPR for protection against unfair competition and all other rights resulting from intellectual activity, literary or artistic fields. It was only in the case of Dr. Rabindranath Tagore that the Central Government enacted laws to protect his works for 50 years after his death and later extended by another 10 years. The Central Government has finally limited the copyright for 60 years only after the death of the author.

Today we live in a world of instant global communications. It is an era of fast technological developments and information technology. In recent times techniques of reproducing documents and access to documents through faster communication has become reality. New techniques for sound recording and visual images have increased. Simple, inexpensive and readily available magnetic tape reproduction equipments with low cost tapes, cassettes have made copying of phonograph records simple. New computer technology has brought a revolutionary change. These technologies are providing unlimited opportunities for communication between people and new tools for teaching. These have helped many people to reproduce documents and other materials illegally on a large scale causing problems to copyright owners and government agencies. A number of laws are being enacted to protect copyrights.

Librarians have an important role in protecting the rights of the patent holders, copyright holders and others in the field of industrial designs, trademarks, trade secrets, layout designers of integrated circuits etc. The librarian should keep themselves aware with the latest changes in I.P.R and to oversee their proper implementation while purchasing books and other materials and also when these are used in the library. It is a social obligation that the librarians have to perform. In the curriculum of Library and Information Science, keeping in view the importance of access to information it should include various issues related to IPR. May be a short-term course in IPR been framed specially for the librarians. It would thus help the society to protect the IP owners from plagiarism, counterfeiting and other malpractices in time of growing information technology, evolution of global media and communication revolution.

2

The Indian Copyright Act And Its Implications To Libraries And Information Centers

A.A.N.Raju

Introduction

The advent of Knowledge Society replacing Agricultural and Industrial Societies has resulted in the emergence of new forms of property, which is the result of human intellect and endeavor. This new form of intellectual property has come to play a vital role in the lives of human beings. The intellectual property primarily consists of trademark, copyright and patent rights apart from trade secrets, publicity rights, moral rights and right against unfair competitions.

Copyright is a unique kind of intellectual property and its importance is growing day by day. It is the human beings who have the capacity of creativity. They can be authors, composers, artists and designers for creating and producing original works. It is they alone who have the exclusive rights to enjoy or they authorize others for certain acts in relation to 1.literary, dramatic, musical and artistic works, and 2. Cinematography film and 3. Sound recordings. The basic areas that are covered under the copyright protection are in the domain of printing, music communication, and entertainment and computer industries.

Object of Copyright Act

In order to protect the rights of authors and artists who create and produce intellectual products various countries of the world have enacted copyright laws and India is no exception in this regard. The copyright acts have been enacted to check the piracy i.e.

infringement of rights so that the fruits of the labor put forth by the author or the copyright owner may be enjoyed by the deserving authors and copy right owners and not the pirates or plagiarists who undermine the rights of intellectual property creators.

The Indian Scenario

The earliest act relating to copyright was the Indian Copyright Act of 1847 enacted during the East India Company Rule. It was passed on 15th December 1847. This was followed by Indian Copyright Act of 1914, which was a modified version of British Copyright act of 1911. The two acts combining together constituted the copyright law in India. The Acts of 1914 provided penalties for the infringement of the copyright, which was not considered as a criminal offense. The said Act authorized the destruction of infringed copies of their delivery.

After India's independence the technological, economic and social changes, which have taken, place in the country necessitated a comprehensive copyright law. The result was the Copyright Act of 1957. This Act introduced several new features, which are as follows:

Establishment of Copyright Office under the control of Registrar of Copyrights who shall act under the directions of the Central Government.

Setting up of Copyright Board which will determine the reasonableness of rates of fees, charges or royalties claimed by performing rights societies. Definition of copyright was enlarged to include the exclusive right to communicate works by radio diffusion. A cinematography film will have separate copyright apart from its various components viz.; story, music etc. An author assigning copyright of his work is allowed the option to acquire the copy right after seven years with certain limitations.

The term to the copyright fixed to be the life of the author and a period of 25 years after his death. A license may be issued to any library to make or cause to be made one copy of any book in which copyright subsists and which is not available for sale. Provisions are made for regulating the activities of performing rights societies and also for controlling the fees, charges or royalties to be collected by them.

Certain rights akin to copyright are conferred on broadcasting authorities in respect to programs broadcast by them. International copyright relations which are based on International treaties shall be regulated by specific orders to be made by Govt. of India.

Amendments to the Act of 1957

The basic features of Indian Copyright act 1957 conform to the provisions of the two International acts viz. 1. Berne Convention and 2. Universal Copyright Convention. India is member of both the conventions, which were revised at Paris in 1971.

The Indian Copyright Act was amended so far four times in the years 1983, 1984, 1994 and 1999 to keep pace with the changing times and requirements of the emerging knowledge society. The 1983 amendment provides for: a) provisions of compulsory licenses for translation and reproduction of foreign work required for instructional purposes, b) providing adequate protection to authors rights and c) removing administrative bottlenecks for administering the Copyright Act of 1957.

As the piracy of the word, sound recordings and cinematograph films increased to unimaginable proportions all the countries enacted stringent laws to curb the menace. India also initiated action in the direction. The 1984 amendment contained the following: 1. Increase the punishment provided for the infringement or violation of the copyright to three years with a minimum of six months and fine up to Rs.2 lakhs with a minimum of Rs.50000. 2. Provision for the declaration of the offence of infringement of copyright as an economic offence and 3. To make provisions of the act applicable to video films and computer programs.

As the anti piracy provisions incorporated in 1984 amendment could not work effectively Govt. of India appointed a Working Group in 1987 to recommend suitable amendments taking into account the rapid advances made in Information and Communication technologies.

As a result of the suggestions of the Working Group and the recommendations of the Joint Committee of the both the houses of the parliament, the copyright act was amended again in 1994. This amendment provides for: 1.performers rights protection covering any visual or artistic presentation made live by one or more performers, 2.Copy right Societies seeking to promote collective administration of rights of authors, composers and other creative artists, 3 assignment of copyright by an author or an artist to protect the interests of both the assigner and assignee and 4. Computer programs, cinematograph and films and sound recordings protection.

The Copyright Act was again amended in the year 1999 which incorporated:

1. Amended definition of literary works,
2. Meaning of copy right in respect of computer program,
3. Increased term of copy right of performers from 25 years to 50 years,
4. New provisions pertaining to power of Govt. of India to apply the provisions relating to Broadcasting Organizations and performance to Broadcasting Organizations.

Extent of Copyright

Section 14 of the Indian Copyright Act provides for the meaning and extent of copyright. It includes literary works, artistic works, dramatics works, musical works and computer software.

The rights in respect of literary works include- to publish/ reproduce, to translate, to adapt and to covert into music/record.

The rights in respect of artistic works include- to perform in public, to broadcast, to adapt/copy, to make a cine film and to create a sound track/recording.

The rights in respect of dramatic works include- to reproduce, to publish, to make a cine film and to adapt.

The rights in respect of musical works in include- to broadcast, to perform publicly, to make sound track/recording and to copy.

The rights in respect of computer software include- to use in literary work, drama, artistic work, music, engineering design, sports and games and others.

Implications to LICs

The Indian Copyright Act protects the authors of their intellectual property rights. At present reprographic service has become a common reader's service in most of our libraries and Information Centers (LICs). Especially in Academic, Special and Research libraries to meet the demands of the user community chapter/s from books, reports, reference books and from many other sources of information and sometimes the entire document from cover to cover is photocopied and made available to the user community.

This is a clear violation of the Indian Copyright Act. As per the provisions of the Act license has to be obtained from the concerned authority for making photocopies available to the user community in case the concerned document is not available for sale. This provision applies only to rare and out of print documents and the period of copyright has not expired or lapsed.

There are instances where some of the Publishing / Bookselling Agencies without proper permission/authority sold photocopied editions of Universal Decimal Classification (UDC) and Dewey Decimal Classification (DDC) schedules at throw away prices. The same fate struck Colon Classification (CC) also. Many of the Library Schools have resorted to the same unethical methods to augment the schedules of classification for teaching practical to a large number of students.

These unauthorized practices is a clear violation of Indian Copyright Act and liable for punishment under the relevant sections of the act. It is the sacred duty of the library profession to protect and safeguard the intellectual property rights of authors, composers, artists and designers.

References

1 The Copy right Act (India), 1957

2 Reddy,G.B. Intellectual Property Rights and the Law, Hyderabad, Gogia Law Agency, 2000.

3

Information, Intellectual Property And The Librarian

M. R. Riswadkar

Today there are unmistakable indications that entire higher education is moving away from a vertical toward a horizontal dimesnsion that transcends traditional disciplinary boundaries to seek a universal function common to all curricula, ——. For the librarian, this trend towards the horizontal is particularly significant because no discipline is more innately interdisciplinary than that which concerns itself with the management and utilization of graphic records, and no knowledge can rightly be regarded as irrelevant to its practice[1]. Numbers 3, 4, 5 requires to be superscript like on P. 16.

According to Shera, "no knowledge can rightly be regarded as irrelevant to" librarianship, for access to all knowledge is the basic objective and function of it. However, the interdisciplinarity of librarianship, if more deeply examined in the light of a profound discussion held at an OECD seminar on the subject in – 1972 at Paris, appears to be indiscriminate.[2] Indiscriminate interdisciplinarity results from the borrowing of concepts, techniques and tools from a multitude of disciplines. Librarianship is considered an enccyclopaedic endeavour, and, as such, must of necessity practise indiscriminate interdisciplinarity, the most recent examples of this being the inclusion of TQM and SWOT analysis in its curricula.

Borrowing concepts developed elsewhere become bolder and more pronounced perhaps after the expansion of library science into library and information science. In the matter of technology, librarianship has covered a very vast expanse from the Council on Library Resources' Library Technology Project of 1964 to now utiquitous OPAC and CD_ROM. Information technology and management science appear to have become most fashionable areas for library science education to create "curriculon mix-ups". These are, however, not the only disciplines from where librarianship has borrowed concepts and techniques from. Bibliometrics owes a lot to statistics; information behaviour to psychology; and vocabulary control to linguistics. The management doctrine of cost-effectiveness perhaps prompted Dr. Urquhart to evolve the principle of providing the existing services at decreased costs or increased services at the existing costs.[3] Dr. Urqurhart's concern is obviousely for output being equal to input where output is service and input is the cost of it. Economics thus comes in as one more fascet of this indiscriminate, interdisciplinary framework of librarianship.

Now, economics, as Kenneth E. Boulding states, is "primarily the science of commodities". To paraphrase Boulding, a commodity is exchanged and has a price. It can be produced and consumed. A commodity is thus created and destroyed. Knowledge also possesses all these properties and can claim to be a commodity.[4] If Boulding discusses knowledge as a commodity, Kenneth Anow discusses information as a commodity.[5] In his opinion, when uncertainty creates a problem in resource allocation, information becomes a commodity (Manfred Kochan, in "Information for action, defines information as that which removes uncertainty; New York, Academic Press, 1975, pp. 1-180). Information will frequently have an economic value. Further, information can become an appropriable commodity with suitable legal measures, e.g. patents. Only appropriable commodities can be exchanged. A patent is exclusive intellectual property. It can therefore be exchanged for money.

Back to Boulding, he differentiates knowledge as a commodity from other commodities in that the former, unlike the latter, does not obey the law of conservation. Here, he gives the example of class-room situation. In a class-room, after the teacher's lecture is over what was earlier known to one is now known to many. According to Boulding, therefore, spread of knowledge is akin to growth of knowledge, while in the matter of other consumables turnover results in the decrease in stock. The point most relevant to librarians Boulding makes in the course of his argument is that commodities are exchanged through middlemen. Boulding regards the librarian and the bibliographer as middlemen contributing to the function of exchange in the world of intellect. Lastly, if pursuit and transmission of knowledge is a specialised function in society it must be paid for.

Both Boulding and Arrow are economists and together they discuss knowledge and information as commodities. However, a word of caution is necessary. With reference to knowledge possessing the properties of commodity, Boulding has used the words "At times——," while in the case of information as a commodity, Arrow's word is "frequently", Logically, "at times" and "frequently" are synonymous terms meaning "not always". Arising from this, one may ask oneself as to when knowledge or information is regarded as a commodity. Arrow has given the answer straight away by saying that when uncertainty creates a problem in resource allocation, information becomes a comodity. Acquisition of books and journals in libraries is a case in point. Boulding, on the other hand, explains this phenomenon rather obliquely. It is already stated above that he likens growth of knowledge to spread of knowledge. "Growth" is one phenomenon. There is another he calls "increase". While teaching, in his view, results in "growth", research results in "increase". He observes, "——— a researcher obtains new knowledge from nature rather than from men or from books". Perhaps this knowledge Boulding regards as a commodity. One may therefore conclude that a patent, it being the outcome of research, is a commodity having an economic value. Since it is "exclusive intellectual propety", it can be exchanged for money. Even in law, property is conveyed for consideration. Let it be granted then that knowledge at times acts as a commodity. What about information ?

In the matter of information, Arrow, it is already seen, is more articulate. In his words, "information frequently has an economic value". Boulding admits that knowledge "clearly is related to information" which one can measure in terms of bits. However, he does not view knowledge as "a mere pile of bits of information".

The appropriate term for a unit of knowledge, he thinks, is "wit" and not "bit". Presumably, therefore, that part of information which signifies wit or intellect is knowledge and to that extent information is a commodity having an economic value.

It is thus obvious that the concept "information as a commodity" is a gift of economics to library and information science. It is an established fact that the profession has accepted the concept and there is nothing wrong in doing it. It is now worthwhile to present here a brief review of the development of this commodity concept in the field of library and information science.

As Carlos Cuadra pointed out, there exists an information industry that sells database services and other products to libraries and information organisations which form what he terms as "information market place". Further, there is an institution called information brokers, big and small, performing custom information services for a fee. Information activities are a business which sustains on a principle that there is no such thing as free information. Information costs something to develop and to disseminate. There are free information services such as public libraries. But these are really not free; they are paid for by taxpayers.[6]

Public sector is as much a part of information industry, e.g. MEDLARS and OCLC. All finances for OCLC's development come from the sale of products and services to participant libraries. OCLC's revenue has been, as it should be, in excess of its operating costs. This excess, known as price in economics, is available for reinvestment in creating new facilities and new services.[7]

Don Swanson advocated fee for extra services, e.g. on-line access. This, he said, would ensure a vital feedback for libraries to know which services are more valued and which are less valued.[8]

According to Peter Watson, as quoted by Swanson, fees are not ethically wrong, or politically unwise. They are not educationally unsound or economically inefficient.

Reference is already made above to Urquhart's principle of cost-effectiveness of library services. Here is another, more relevant in the present context: Libraries have to be paid for.[9]

Librarians then go alongwith the economists that information is a commodity and it costs to produce it. The cost of information is the sum of human and non-human resources involved in originating, handling and distributing it. Information products thus acquire an economic value and so are priced. Librarians are aware of the existence of laws that recognise the status of economic goods of information products.

Arising from the foregoing discussion it is clear that intellectual property is manifest in patents and books. The patent law and Copyright Act ensure protection of this property. There are international organisations to safegurd the interests of researchers and authors. Librarians are particularly concerned with the Copyright Act. Since they have accepted the concept "information as a comodity', they should, and do, honour the provisions in the Copyright Act. They should, and do, ensure that the photocopying services provided in their libraries serve the purpose of only study and research. This is their moral obligation devolved on them because, as Boulding sees, they are "middlemen contributing to the function of exchange in the world of intellect".

References

1. Jesse H. Shera. The foundations of education for librarianship. New York, Becker and Hayes, 1972. p. 327.
2. Heinzs Heckhausen. "Discipline and interdisciplinarity" in Inerdisciplinarity: problems of teaching and research in universities. Paris, OECD, 1972. pp. 83-89.
3. D. J. Urquhart. The principles of librarinahip. Bardsey, Leeds, Wood Garth, 1981. p 100.
4. Kenneth E. Boulding. "Knowledge as a commodity" in Beyond economcis. Ann Arbor, Univeristy of Michigan Press, 1970. pp. 141-155.
5. Kenneth Arrow. in Economics of information and knowledge, ed. By Donald Lamberton. Penguin Books, 1971.
6. Carlos Caudra. "The role of the private sector in the development and improvement of library and information services." Library Quarterly, 50:1, 1980, 94-111.

7. ———. in The on-line revolution in libraries, ed. by Allen Kent and Thomas J. Gavin. New York, Marcel Dekker. 1978, 53-61.

8. Don Swanson R. "Evolution, libraries and national information policy" Library Quarterly, 50:1, 1980,76-93.

9. D. J. Urquhart. Op. cit.

4

'FAIR USE' DOCTRINE AND COPYRIGHT

P.S.G. Kumar

Copyright

Till recently most people thought that they could use and enjoy the writings of an author, the music of a composer and the paintings of an artist freely without realising that the creater had to be compensated. In the modern world where every thing has acquired by paying some amount of compensation to the owner, the fact that a creative work has also to be paid for, is much less understood in developing countries than in advance countries.

Although copyright is an old concept, the question of evolving a system of copyright profession become a live issue only after the advent of printing with the advent of audio-visual media, development of digital storage and communication technologies, the concept of copyright and protection of intellectual property rights on one hand become important and on the other more complex to monitor and regulate.

Fair Use

The term 'fair use' is a term used in USA. In UK it is called 'fair dealing'. It is interesting to note that the term 'fair use' has never been defined in law. It is left to the courts (in the event of a dispute) to decide what may be 'fair' and what amounts to infringement.

Bench – Marks

The Bench –Marks generally used for deciding fair use are:

a. Effect of copying on the potential market for the work.

b. The number of copies made out of the original.

c. The purpose for which copying has been done-Research or private study; or commercial research; and

d. Extent of copying – reasonable or substantial.

Effect on markets

Fair use is normally regarded as a possible means of covering any action, which should not unduly affect a rights owner's market. Movements were there world over to protect and preserve the 'fair use' concept which permits the users to copying of a portion of a document – book, periodical article, phonorecord, video, database etc; and reproduce the original work for a specific purpose and to a limited extent. Except library copying permission (which are specific and unchallangeble) anything done under fair use is potentially subject to challenge by rights an owner on grounds of fairness.

Number of copies made

Most of the copyright conventions allow reproduction of a single copy of the journal article. However the British Copyright Council (BCC) argues. "Libraries are given the right to operate the library privileges and very strict conditions, suggests strongly that fair dealing does not encompass in any way the copying of an entire article from a periodical".

However it is to be noted that no Act has prescribed any limit for fair use. The prescriptions are loose- mainly based on the concept of 'non-profit' and 'reasonable bounds for the sake of rights owners'. The advent of commercial database complicated the accepted concept of 'fairness'.

Purpose of copying

The Association of Learned and Professional Society Publishers (ALPSP), (UK) considered journal article copying to be fair dealing for research or private study and may continue, so for other than databases. The copyright acts tried to distinguish between 'research or private study' and ' commercial or profit oriented'.

Concessions are liberally granted for research and private

study, where as, much restricted to commercial research organizations and individuals. Though, limits of use are demarcated, copyright acts are mostly silent over provisions, procedures and penalties. Things are left to the courts of law.

Extent of copying

The British Copyright Council states the views of the Society of Authors, the Writers Guild and the Publishers Association; that in general the following are considered fair dealing for research or private study copying by individuals. Some BCC views have been augmented as indicated.

Books and other non-periodical material

a. One copy of a maximum of a complete chapter in a book, or one copy of a maximum otherwise of 5 per cent of a literary work. This means whichever is the grater may be copied. As this offers no guidance on short works without chapters, the advice repeated in the Library Association guides is:

b. Short books, reports, standards, and pamphlets: up to 10 per cent if not more than 20 pages or 2 pages if brief. Poems, essays, short stories, etc. It is however pointed out, in respect of anthologies and other cases of inclusion that poems, short stories, and other short literary works must be seen as whole works in them, and not as parts of volumes in which they may appear. In such cases of inclusion in volumes:

c. One copy may be made of a short story or poem, which does not exceed the pages in length. Otherwise, the 5 per cent limit applies. The BCC extents specifically exclude periodical articles, which the BCC regards as whole works in them, although it is mentioned that some journal publishers print permission in each issue for single copying of articles. However, the Association of Learned and Professional Society Publishers indicated a decade ago that it regarded the copying of single periodical articles as fair dealing. No rights-owner guidance is yet available on database right.

Periodicals

When wishing to copy from any periodical, the issue should first be checked at front and back to see if there is any note indicating how copies can be made- and, if necessary, paid for- when the requirement exceeds the extent and single copy obtainable legally from a nonprofit-based library service. If the payment is to be made to an overseas address, this is not practical because the bank transfer charges would probably exceed the charged, but a photocopy could be requested via the nearest library from the British Library Document Supply Center or another agency which is licensed to copy in excess of singles and more than the 'one article per issue' limit. Certain Concessions Under British copyright the permitted purpose to which the 'fair dealing' concept (ss 29,30) came into application from 1st January 1998 are:

a. From s29: research or private study- applicable to any original work, including artistic work, and including copying of a "typographical arrangement' (printed page), but not to extraction or re-utilization (by whatever means) of parts of databases for research having a commercial purpose;

b. From s30:

   i. criticism or review of any copyright work, or of a performance of a work subject to sufficient acknowledgment;

   ii. News reporting (i.e. current events) in respect of any copyright work except a photography, subject to sufficient acknowledgment when the news is being reported in written or printed form: provided neither (i) or (ii) involves the extraction or re-utilization of the whole or a substantial part of a database, because s30 is not reflected under database right.

Within the permitted purposes, 'fair dealing' can range over all possible treatments of copyright material which otherwise might amount to infringement. Thus fair dealing under (1) could override considerations of the 'substantial part' which would otherwise infringe.

Under (1), copying is possible from a database for research or private study if the purpose is not commercial, or if the parts concerned are defensibly 'insubstantial' whatever the purpose.

Since the fair dealing concept is really only a permissible defence if taken to court for infringement, anything done under fair dealing obviously calls for the exercise of judgment. So it is advisable to take due note of any guidelines issued by rights-owner groups in order to indicate what they regard as 'fair'. The 'moral rights' must also be borne in mind when considering whether a given action might be accepted as fair.

Criticism or review

For criticism or review, any copyright work, or a performance of a work, is covered. This includes, for example, films and sound recordings. Any reproduction must be accompanied by sufficient acknowledgement. Copying or quoting a sufficient extent or significance to be judged 'fair' in court. Obviously it would be most unfair to include large quantities of a work, since serious harm could result to the rights owner's market, for which due recompense would probably be sought in the courts this should be borne in mind not only by reviewers but also by the producer of an abstract, digest or precis: for example, a 'full' precis should only be published with permission.

Quotation limits

In 1958, the Society of Authors and the Publishers Association jointly agreed that while the limits of 'fair dealing' for the purpose of criticism or review must vary according to the circumstances, it would be a convenience to all concerned and save correspondence about short quotations for these purposes if a general understanding could be established for normal practice.

They therefore would not regard it as 'unfair' if a single extract of 400 words, or a series of extracts (of which none exceeded 300 words) to a total of 800 words were taken from prose copyright works, or... Up to 40 lines from a poem. Provided that this extract amounted to no more than one quarter of the poem.

Quoted from photocopying and the law, British Copyright Council, 1970 reprint of 1960s pamphlet; excluded from the Bibliography because it has been withdrawn in the light of new law and the inception of licensing. This particular statement, however, has not been revised and should still be followed in general as the only advice available, subject to possible review in the light of database right. Under database right, as indicated earlier, anyone may extract or re-utilize an insubstantial part of a database for any purpose without infringement, through deciding what might be accepted as 'insubstantial' will need assistance from rights-owner guidelines in due course, or from case law.

Discretion is important, however, in ensuring that a quotation is not excessive unless authorized, and particularly in seeking permission for any 'advertisement or marketing' applications irrespective of permitted use for 'criticism or review'. More rights must also be borne in mind: for example, a falsely credited or unrepresentative quotation could cause considerable offence and lead to litigation.

Multiple copying, or publication, is not ruled out for criticism or review by CDPA88 provided sufficient acknowledgement is made. It is advised however that one should not assume this to be applicable to multiple copying or re-publication of any part of a printed page, because typographical arrangement is not specifically cleared for this purpose, unlike research or private study. However the British Photographers' Liason Committee guide accepts that a photograph may be reproduced for criticism or review, either on its own or as part of a compilation of several authors' works, provided that it is accompanied by a credit identifying the author and title, if any. Quotation for criticism or review is in any event legally subject to sufficient acknowledgement of source. Excessive quotation requirements- and any other purpose than the two specifically allowed- should be the subject of permission requests. Response to requests to newspapers may vary according to whether an item has an individual by-line.

Efforts to Protect Fair Use in USA

The Digital Millennium Copyright Act (1998) threatened the

traditional fair use rights of users of intellectual property in USA. Republication Rick Boucher has announced that he will introduce legislation to protect fair use for libraries and scholars. He said: " The time, in my opinion, has come, for the Congress to reaffirm the fair use doctrine, and to bolster specific fair use rights, which are now at risk," Boucher said at a March 6 conference sponsored by the Consumer Electronic Association. In his speech (a transcript of which has been posted on the Tech Law Journal's Web site at www.techlawjournal.com/intelpro/20010306boucher.asp), Boucher cited predictions that under Section 1201 of the law," what is available today on the library shelves for free will be available on a pay- per-sue basis only". He suggested that the law be amended to prohibit the circumvention of electronic encryption devices only for infringement purpose; barring that, he suggested crafting a more limited amendment to protect fair use rights of libraries and scholars.

Boucher, a senior member of the House Courts, Internet, and Intellectual Property Subcommittee, also proposed measures to extend broadcast copyright exemptions for distance learning to proposal computers and the Internet, and to ensure that the first-sale doctrine applies to online sales of copyrighted material.

Also at the conference, Senate Judiciary Committee Chair Orrin Hatch has reportedly called for market-oriented solutions to concerns over the DMCA, which he co-authored, rather than amendments to the law.

Conclusion

The issues are thus becoming more complicated with pricing of information in electronic media and thus the whole issue of copyright is being reviewed all over the world. As regards to the use of books and issues pertaining to libraries, the existing norms, conventions and regulations are to be kept in mind.

References

1. Wall, R. A. Copyright made easier, Ed 2. London: Aslib, 1998.567p.
2. American Libraries, April 2001. p16.

5

Copyright and Library Service

S. R. Ganpule

The response to the copyright issue from the developing countries is that it is a new device articulated by developed countries for exploitation of the former. While this may be true in the other components of the Intellectual Property Rights of which copyright has been made a part, it does not appear to be an instrument for exploitation but a measure for protection and promotion of creativity in the society. While the western societies give more emphasis on economic aspect of the copyright issue, the eastern societies, particularly Indian society look to the moral aspect. This is because of the tradition in which the creative works flourished in this country.

In India the creative works in the form of literature, music, art and sculpture generated as a service to the God. In India the creative works were created in the spirit of 'Idam Na Mama' ('This Is Not Mine') or Brahmarpanmastu (Be It At The Feet Of The Eternal Power). Naturally the economic aspects got secondary, if not a, place in the process of creation. Even then the right of ownership was ensured when literary works like devotional songs ended with the author's citation in the last line (symbolically like 'Baparakhumadevivaru' or directly like 'Tuka mhane', 'Nama mhane') Perhaps, this may be because the economic aspect was taken care of either by the kings who patronized them or by devotees who followed them. Where the religious feelings were very strong the creative works (like Ajanta sculptures) remained without the name of the creator. Moreover, since such works formed the part of knowledge (Vidya), they were to be spread without charging the fees. This tradition prevailed right up to advent of the British period, or even during most part of the British period.

Even after the independence the influence of this tradition prevailed. As at today except in the case of books of popular authors, which are very much in demand (such as text books, popular novels, well received dramas) the copyright in case of literary works is in the name rather than in action.

In the days ahead when the world will come closer and closer, the interaction with other countries will increase and the IPR will become part of our daily life, copyright, which forms as a part of IPR will have to be taken due care of. We have already done it by signing the WTO convention and passing the copyright act. The visible effect of it will be seen in the days to come.

Despite the tradition, the economic aspect of copyright has to be given due importance by us because the economic aspect serves two purposes. In one way, it provides economic benefits to the artist, who is essential for his worldly life; in the other, it encourages him to continue performing and performing better. They also provide, indirectly incentives to other artists – the real purpose behind the provision of the protection of right.

We are all aware of the nature of copyrights. We are aware about three international conventions and the Copyright Acts passed by individual countries within the framework of the provisions of these conventions. To be familiar with this is necessary for librarians. It is necessary to know which rights are protected and how to operate under this provision. It is not the purpose of this paper to go into the details of this provision because it will be repetition of what other papers have said. The purpose of this paper is to discuss the effect of these provisions on the traditional library services that are being rendered by librarians.

The rights that are affecting the traditional library services, directly or indirectly are:

- The rights to copy a work
- To Issue copies to the public
- To rent or lend the work

Other rights viz. to perform, show or play the work, to broadcast the work and to adapt the work are not directly related to library service, except in special case the right to perform, show or play may be related to the extension activities of library.

Protection against lending the books does affect the library service, as lending of books is a core function of the library. As far as the lending in the parental libraries is concerned the protection is not affecting the lending service because in such libraries, - school college, universities and the libraries attached to parent organization – the lending is restricted to the members and not public at large. As long as selling the books to libraries is not restricted the right of the library to lend the books to the members – does not affect the protection. In theoretical terms, the moral right of the authors do get protected.

The authorship is recognized and the purpose for which the work is created serves more forcefully. In the case of public libraries, however to some extent the protection does get affected as the public libraries have to loan to the public at large. The Public Lending Rights is the answer to this problem. Of course, the implementation depends upon the efficient management of public library service. In an unorganized state, such as in our country, realization of gains of Public Lending Rights is a difficult proposition. Anyway when they get property organized the PLR may prove to be an effective solution

Major concern in all types of library service is relating to copying of the work. The provisions relating to copying are:

a. Substantive part of the work cannot be copied,

b. Only one article (content page is considered as one article) from a periodical issue can be copied,

c. Ownership of copyright of the books, which is out of print needs to be traced when copying from it, is needed.

Like the lending function, the dissemination of the information is an inherent function of the library. As far as providing information is concerned, no protection of copyright comes in the way except the current content service where exact reproduction of contents page is involved. However if the ultimate purpose of the library is to disseminate the information proper (which finally is what reader wants) the copying from books, journals and other types of reading material is needed. The protection under the copyright affects very seriously in this respect. The surrogates of the matter such as bibliographical entries, or the abstracts or packaged information in the form of digests, trend reports or the progress reports do not serve the purpose. When the library gets, (that, too, after long struggle) only one original of the reading material and the number of the users is large and spread around geographically, taking copies in more than one number is the need of the day for every librarian. Under these circumstances, the only recourse that librarians can take is under the provision of "fair use" or "fair deal". If the definition of the fair deal is stretched to the fullest extent that 'copying does not harm the interest of the owner but benefits the individual and the society ' the librarians can get over the problem to some extent. For example, the books, which are out of print, can be copied in a reasonable number, which will be related to the demand. Say, for instance, it fifty students of undergraduate course are constantly demanding a book which is out of print but is essential for passing the examination, at least three copies should be allowed to be photocopied and allowed for use in the library premises only. Another example can be cited in case of a periodical article. An article which is core to a conference, which will be participated by, say, hundred people for one week should be downloaded on the local network for two weeks – one week prior to conference and one week during the conference. Its further downloading will, of course, be locked.

Even in the case of treating the content page as an article in a periodical the protection should be extended to copy it in more numbers (not of course indefinite) but for use within an organization. This, it will be readily agreed, will be in the interest of both the authors and publishers of periodicals.

Next issue that is concerned with copyright is the preservation of material. By definition libraries are the repositories of knowledge and one of their basic functions is to preserve the past knowledge for posterity and preserve it in such as way that it can be easily communicated. This requires copying either in a more durable material or by converting in an electronic form. Whereas the Tunish model allows only non-commercial libraries to copy for preservation, the copying activity cannot overlook problems in copying in electronic form.

Copying in electronic form is in a way, a new creation. Although the test of originality, which is the 'sweat of the brow', cannot apply here some interest or skill can be claimed to make it 'original'. Moreover, if the copying can be done by the library or the contractor by using their own machinery, they will own the copyright. In such case, the authors can be at a loss.

In our country, where not many books are read, not many books are purchased, not many patents are obtained, and knowledge is being considered as a thing to be spread by every means the copyright is not a major issue of concern to librarians, as at today or in the near future. However, one cannot ignore it totally. Especially in view of the fact that libraries will go more and more electronic, which surely has an international dimension, will have to be alert about the complicacies of the copyright laws belonging to them.

6

WHAT IS COPYRIGHT?

U. S. Thakare

1. In ancient days creative writers, *musicians and artists wrote, composed or made their works* for fame and recognition rather than to earn a living. The question of copyright never arose because copying was a laborious and expensive process. The importance of copyright was recognised only after the invention of printing in the 15th century, which enable the reproduction of books, in large numbers practicable. Copyright is one form of what is described today as "intellectual property". The general principles of copyright is reflected in article 27 of the Declaration of Human Rights:

   i. Every one has the right freely to participate in the cultural life of the community, to enjoy the arts and to share in scientific advancement and benefits.
   ii. Every one has the right of protection of the moral and material interests resulting from any scientific, literary or artistic production of which he is the author

The very foundation and philosophy of copyright law does not permit one to appropriate to himself what has been produced by the labour, skill and capital of another.

2. Copyright is the right of literary property as recognised and sanctioned by positive law. It is an intangible, incorporeal right granted by statute to the author or originator of certain literary or artistic production, whereby he is inverted, for a limited period, with the sole and exclusive privilege of multiplying copies of the same and publishing and selling them. International copyright is the right of a subject of one country for protection against the republication in another country of a work, which he originally published in his own country.

3. The Copyright Act 1957 has been enacted to amend and consolidate the law relating to copyrights in India. The object of the law is to facilitate, encourage and motivate artists, composers, software programmers, etc. to create original works by a system of granting exclusive right for a limited consumption of the public. After the expiry of the specified period; the work will belong to the public domain and one may reproduce them without permission. Thus the producer of an original work is enabled to prevent others form creating or reproducing his work and in this sense, the author gets the monopoly right in his favour. With the growth of science and technology as well as with the growth in inventive and creative flourish in various aspects of literary, artistic, musical and other arts, the need for copyright protection has become all the more important.
4. In fact, by definition, copyright means the exclusive right to do or authories others to do certain acts in relation to literary, dramatic, music work, artistic work, cinematographic film and records. The importance of copyright was recognised only after the print media was invented about five centuries back, which enable reproduction of books and literatures in large numbers. Logically, the Indian copyright law followed the British Law on the subject.
5. Our government though committed to protect the interests of artists of Indian culture and literature, is to adapt the rapidly changing global economical trade scenario. In this backdrop, the 1957 Act was recently amended by the Copyright (Amended) Act, 1999 seeking to extend the term of protection of performer's right from twenty-five years to fifty years. The Amendment Act provides for powers to government to extend the provisions of the Act to broadcasts and performances made in other countries provided those countries give reciprocal protection to broadcasts and performances made in India.

6. Copyright derives from the expression of "copies of words". The Oxford English Dictionary defines "copyright" as "the exclusive right given by law for a certain term of years to an author, composer etc. or his assignee to print, publish and sell copies of his original work. The Copyright Act affords protection to a much wider species of works. The scope of protection is also wider.
7. In Colliers' Encyclopedia (1956 Edition) copyright is defined as ' as a privilege or franchise granted by the government to authors, composers and artists, which entitles them to the exclusive right of printing or otherwise multiplying, publishing and vending copies of the copyrighted literary or artistic production.
8. Statutory definition of copyright is incorporated in section 14 of copy Right Act 1957. Copyright means the exclusive right to do or authorise others to do certain acts in relation to
   i. Literary, dramatic or musical works
   ii. Computer programme
   iii. Artistic work
   iv. Cinematograph film
   v. Sound recording

The nature of the acts vary according to the subject matter. Basically copyright means the right to copy or reproduce the work in which copyright subsists. The various acts for which copyright extends is listed in section 14 of copy right Act. Since the section begins with the expression "copyright means" it would appear that the definition is exhaustive and copyright does not extend to any right beyond the scope of section 14. The exclusive right for doing the respective acts extends not only to the whole to the work, but to any substantial part thereof or to any translation or adaptation thereof.

9. No copyright exists in and work except as provided under section 16 of the Act. This makes it clear that under the present law copyright is a creation of the statute and there is no such thing recognised as common law copyright. Further

copyright subsists only in the items of work specified in section 13 namely (a) original literary, dramatic musical and artistic work (b) cinematograph film and (c) sound recording.

10. Copyright subsists only in certain works. The term "work" means any of the following, namely (i) a literary, dramatic, musical or artistic work, (ii) a cinematograph film (iii) a record. "Government work" means a work which is made or published by or under the directive or control of (i) the Government or any department or Government, (ii) any Legislature in India, (iii) any court, tribunal or other judicial authority in India.

11. The object of copyright law is to encourage authors, composers and artists to create original works by rewarding them with the exclusive right for a limited period to reproduce the works for the benefit of the public. On the expiry of the term of copyright the works belong to the public domain and anyone may reproduce them without permission. The exclusive right given to the author is a negative right, that is to say, a right to prevent others from copying or reproducing the work.

12.A In order to secure copyright protection what is required is that the author must have bestowed upon the work sufficient judgment, skill and labour or capital. It is immaterial whether the work is wise or foolish, accurate or inaccurate, or whether it has or has not any literary merit.

12.B Copyright is a right given to or derived from works, and it is not a right in novelty of ideas. It is based on the right of an author, artist or composer to prevent another person copying an original work whether it is a book, tune or picture, which he himself has created. There is nothing in the nation of copyright to prevent a second person from producing an identical result provided it is arrived at by an independent process.

13. There is no copyright in ideas. Copyright is an incorporeal property. Since there can be no copyright in ideas or information, it is no infringement of copyright to adopt the ideas of another or to publish information derived from another, provided there

is no copying of the language in which those ideas have, or that information has been previously embodied. Copyright gives protection only to the form and not to the idea.

14. Where a person had written the story scenario and dialogue of a film at the instance of its producer and had been paid valuable consideration therefor, it was the film producer and not the other person who become the first owner of the film, including its story scenario and dialogue.

15. In leading case of *Bunny Reuben and others Petitioners Vs B.J. Panchal and another respondents* (2000(2) mh.L.J.169) Hon'ble Justic S.S.Parkar of Bombay High Court laid down following law:

"Photographs taken for valuable consideration. Photographer would not be first owner of copyright in photographs. If the photographs are taken for valuable consideration at the instance of any person such person and not the photographer in the absence of any agreement to the contrary, would be the first owner of the copyright in the photographs."

16. Showing video films over cable T.V. Network to various subscribers without obtaining licence amounts to broadcasting video films to the public and therefore, it infringes the copyright of the assignees of the copyright in relative to cinematograph films.

References

1 Narayan, P. Copyright law.

2 Civil court manual (Central Acts) Vol. 15.

3 Decided cases of Bombay High Court, Calcutta High Court and Mysore High Court.

7

Copy Right Act In Pre-information Technology

S. K. Kulkarni

If we take present era of information technology as a base, Copy Right Act has got deep roots, in the regime of British Rule. Earlier, there was Copy Right Act, 1911 of United Kingdom. It was modified by Indian Copy Right Act, 1914. Thereafter, in the year 1957, new Act was enacted, because the old Act was not containing law on the subject of copy right in the light of growing public consciousness of rights and obligations of authors and in the light of experience gained in working of the existing law during the previous years. New and advanced means of communications, like broadcasting, litho-photography were developed. So also India declared itself as sovereign, socialist democratic Republic by adopting the constitution of India. Therefore, a complete revision of law of copyright was seemed inevitable. It has introduced several new features, some of them are as under.

i. Copy Right Office was established under the immediate control of Registrar of Copy Rights. He is kept under superintendent of the Central Government. He has to maintain Register of Copyrights.

ii. To encourage registration of Copy right, provision was made that no proceeding regarding infringement of copy right shall be instituted unless copy right is registered in copy right office.

iii. Provision is made for setting up a copy right Board which will determine the reasonableness of the rates of fees, charges of royalties claimed by performing rights societies, consider applications for general licenses for public performances of works and will assess compesation payable in certain circumstances. Order passed by the Board is made appealable before High Court.

iv. Definition of "Copy Rights" was expanded to include the right to communicate works by radio-diffusion.

v. An author assigning copy right in his work was allowed the option to re-acquire the copy right after seven years, but before ten years assignment on the condition to return the amount received by him at the time of assignment with interest thereon.

vi. Normal term of copy right reduced up to life of author and 25 years after his death, then up to life and 50 years.

vii. Provision was made for issue of a general or special license for public performances of any work by means of radio - receiving set of a mechanical contrivance.

viii. Provision was made to issue licence to library to prepare one copy of the book, which is not available in market.

ix. International copy right relations, which are based on treaties to be regulated by specific orders of the Central Government.

x. A fair report of dealing of work for radio summary or judicial proceedings would not constitute infringement of copyright.

2. Thereafter again in the year 1983, the Act was amended to adhere to the revised conventions held on copy right at Peris in the year 1971. India, being a member of the conventions, namely, Barne Convention for the Protection of Literary and Artistic Works (1938) and Universal Copyright Convention (1952), it became necessary to amend the Act to get the benefit of revised conventions. Similarly, it was felt necessary to amend the law as some lacunae were found especially in relation to the protection of author's rights. There was also no provision in the Act for publication of unpublished work of an Indian author, who is either dead or unknown or whose whereabouts are not traceable or where owner of copy right can not be located.

3. New amendments provided compulsory licensing for the translation of a foreign work after expiry of three years from publication of work or after expiry of a period of one year if such publication is to be used for the purpose of teaching, scholarship or research. It has, further, provided compulsory licensing of the reproduction of any edition of foreign literary, scientific or artistic work for the purposes of systematic instructional activities, if after expiry of certain period from the date of the first publication of the edition, the copies are not available in India. Most significant provision made by new amendment is regarding unknown or deceased author. In the case of unpublished works, where the author is either dead or unknown or whereabouts of owner of copy right can not be traced, any person, wishing to publish the material or a translation thereof, can advertise his proposal and thereafter apply to the Copy Right Board for permission. The Board, while granting permission, would fix an approximate royalty. The royalty could be deposited in the public Account of India or any other suitable place or specific period, so that in the event of the owner of the copyright becoming known, he could claim it. It is also provided that, in case of unpublished work of Indian author is desirable to publish in national interest then the legal representatives of such author, who is dead, would be given reasonable period to publish the work. If the L.Rs. fail to publish, the copyright board would publish such work on payment of royalty.
4. Amendment made in the year 1984 was for controlling piracy. Problem of piracy in copyright was first discussed in the Lok - Sabha and measures were suggested by the members. Accordingly, punishment for infringement of copy right was increased up to imprisonment up to three years and fine up to Rs. 2 lacks, with minimum of imprisonment up to six months and fine up to Rs. 50,000/-. Thus, no court can award sentence less than imprisonment up to six months and fine up to Rs. 50,000/-. Similarly, for second and subsequent offences

the punishment provided is more than the first offence. At the same time, offence of infringement of copy right is now considered as economic offences, by virtue of this amendment. Therefore, the limitation for taking cognizence of offence provided in Sec. 469 of Criminal Procedure Code, is now not applicable to the offence.

5. In the year 1992, the term of copy right was extended upto 60 years from fifty, from the death of author, in view to protect the copy right vested in "Visva Bharati" in respect of the published works of Gurudeo Ravindranath Tagore. The term was extended as the works of Shri Tagore is considered to be of national importance.

6. What is infringement of copyright is dealt by section 51 of the Act. Law to determine infringement is developed by various precedents. While deciding infringement, the result of the act is taken into consideration and not intention. It is taken as invasion of a right to property, therefore, the intention of the infringer is immaterial.

7. But what is infringement? The question is answered by Hon'ble Lordships of Karnataka High Court by laying down, what is called as "lay observer test". In Associate Electronics and Electrical Industries (Bangalore) Pvt. Ltd., v/s. M/s. Sharp Tools, (AIR 1991 Karn, 406) the appealant, Associate Electronics, had filed an application to cancel the copy right granted to the respondent sharp tools, with copy right Board, The appellant was manufacturer of electronic and electrical goods by trade mark "Sharp", which was registered with Trade and Merchandise Marks Act, 1958. The respondent was manufacturer of engineering equipments such as motors, pump-sets, Jigs etc. But they used trade name "Sharp Tools" while marketing the same. The appellant stated that it is infringement of its right. Hon'ble lordships observed:

"There can be no copy right in the word, but the right can only be in the artistic manner in which the same is written. One of the surest test to determine whether or not there has been a violation of copyright is to see if the reader, spectator, or the viewer after having read or seen both the works would be clearly of the opinion and get an unmistakable impression that the subsequent work appears to be a copy of the first. In other words, dealing with the question of infringement of copy right of the artistic work, the court has to test on the visual appearance of the object and drawing, design, or artistic work in question and by applying the test viz. 'the lay observer test' whether to persons who are not experts in relation to objects of the description, the object appear to be a reproduction. If to the 'lay observer', it would not appear to be reproduction, there is no infringement of the artistic copyright in the work.

However, this principle is in turn based upon the observations of Hon'ble Lordships of Supreme Court in *R. G. Anand V/s. M/s. Delux Films (AIR 1978 S.C. 1613).*

There can be no copyright in an idea, subject-matter, themes, plots or historical or legendary facts and violation of the copyright in such cases is confined to the form, manner and arrangement and expression of the idea by the author of the copyrighted work. Where the same idea is being developed in a different manner, it is manifest that the source being common similarities are bound to occur. In such cases courts should determine whether or not the similarities are on fundamental or substantial aspects of the mode of expression adopted in the copyrighted work, If the defendant's work is nothing but a literal imitation of the copyrighted work with some variations here and there it would amount to violation of the copyright. In other words, in order to be actionable the copy must be a substantial and material one which at once leads to the conclusion that the defendant is guilty of an act of piracy."

8. Once infringement is proved, action for damages or injunction or any other as contemplated under or injunction or any other as contemplated under the Act is bound to be there. Even honest and concurrent user of the copyright is no defence available under the Act. The point is made clear by Hon'ble Lordships of Supreme Court in M/s. Power Control Appliances

and others V/s. Sumeet Machines Pvt. Ltd. (1994) 2 S.C.C.488) In this case, power control was manufacturer of kitchen mixies under brand name "Sumeet". The mixy was packed in a cardboard box and to the top the pictorial and photograph display of the appliance in different colours showing different purposes for which the mixy could be used was shown. A booklet was enclosed bearing the title "Sumeet domestic Mixer-Operating Instructions and Recipe book", with guarantee card. The plaintiff power control contended that, it has owned the copy right with respect to all above items as per section 17. The defendant, which mainly was manufacturer of washing machines and vacuum cleaners, started manufacturing mixies, exactly similar to plaintiff with similar packing material. The defendant contended that it is with honest and concurrent user of the same because it was with consent of one of the directors of plaintiff company. Hon'ble Lordships said "Such user is no defence available under Sec. 51 of the Act. Hence can not be accepted."

9. Thus, the copyright Act has undergone several changes taking into consideration the need of the people and international conventions. Now it has become again necessary to amend it taking into consideration the globalization and development of information and technology faculty. Piracy in respect of computer software has increased. There is no protection to the software prepared and one can easily pirate the same. Pictures and programmes loaded in computers can also be downloaded easily.

10. Concept of intellectual property right is also emerging in India. Since the GATT agreement, people in our country have also become conscious about this right. We have successfully tackled with the problem of turmeric patent, neem patent. Basmati patent etc. Some of our products have obtained international standards. But still we are not recognizing intellectual right of a doctor, a legal practitioner, an engineer, architect etc. In fact, these persons acquire special knowledge in their fields

and it is their property. Copyright is also a kind of intellectual property right. We have recognised it and regulerised the enforcement of it by enacting a law. But there is no law to protect the right of a doctor, an advocate or an engineer. Still we are encouraging consultation with these persons free of costs. It can not be disputed that poor persons should get the help from these experts free of costs or on subsidised rates. But why it should be expected from all lawyers to provide legal aid free of costs?

11. Computer hardware, equipment, functional components have been traditionally protected by granting patents. But field of software is considered to be a field of literary work and therefore it is protected by copyright. Copyright is granted to the creators of original works of authorship. In our country, recently, Information and Technology Act, 2000 has been enacted to authenticate the information received by the use of the computers or to regulate the e-commerce. It has suitably amended Indian Penal Code. Indian Evidence Act, Banker's Books Evidence Act and the Reserve Bank of India Act. However, the Act is not providing for protecting softwares.

Thus, to protect softwares by copyright and also to recognize the rights of intellectuals as intellectual property is a need of to-days.

Section 2

IPR and Information Technology

8

Copyright Status of Digital Information Systems In Libraries

Dominic. J
Nirmala. P. J

Introduction

The time in which we live is often referred to as the information age. In this age information is considered as a resource that has no value until extracted, processed and utilized. The amount of information generated today is astronomical and the problems relating to its storage, dissemination and analysis are testing human ingenuity. Fortunately, new technologies are being developed at an extraordinary rate and this ensures an exciting contest between generation and utilization of information. It is obvious that the new technology will have considerable impact in the copyright law and there will be consequent burden on the information users. Further, it is necessary to give a brief idea about copyright law in the context of electronic publishing. Copyright is a right of ownership similar to the ownership of a house. The object of the text of a book, for instance – is a perceptible object like the house, and both can be bought, sold, inherited, willed and leased, but in both cases the ownership itself is an intangible idea. Copyright protection is not confined to books only. It extends to sound recordings, films, and programmes broadcast by radio and television. Protection is not confined to works which are artistic in the critics sense. Codes are copyrightable, and so is a child's first writing. Virtually in, every country of the world, copyright is an automatic right – one does not have to register with some central authority and indeed, even putting © is not essential, although it is helpful and convenient.

Implication of copyright law on databases

The law of copyright were framed in order to protect an author against piracy of his work. This right is not a right which arises under common law, but is a right which has arisen by statutory protection. Hence, if one is to be granted by this right, one would have to examine the statutory framework under which the laws of copyright were enacted.

Today worldwide explosion of information and revolution of communication, many interesting issues have come up which have great impact in the field of library and information science. Library professionals and information scientists are the information providers to the information seekers or the information user community. In doing so, they use various sources of information. They often download required information from online and CD-ROM databases. Copyright law on data base producers, online hosts, and users of online hosts and CD-ROM does not provide clear cut solutions relating to their piracy, unauthorized users, etc. This is because the concept of database is not understood by legislators. This ambiguity crops up scope for debate about whether data bases are indeed literary works or compilations. Most electronic databases, whether comprising words or numbers, will be considered in most legislations as compilations. It is necessary to define compilation at this stage. A typical definition has been taken from the US copyright Act and is mentioned below:

"A compilation is work formed by the collection and assembling of preexisting material, or of data that are selected, co-ordinate, or arranged in such a way that the resulting work as a whole constitutes an original work of authorship".

Production through copyright laws

Three broad approaches used for database protection are

1. **Protection of Databases Through Contracts**

   Protection of databases through contracts permits a user to use the database under a license from the database owner on payment of a fee, based upon the amount of usage and /

or royalty. License does not pass the ownership of the database to the user. A contract may be used in addition to the protection of database under the copyright laws.

2. **Database Protection Through Copyright Laws**

Most countries have accorded protection to databases under the copyright laws. Definitions of databases and legal interpretations of the protection under copyright vary considerably from one country to another. The question of intellectual skills involved in the creation of databases has been debated. Many databases do not qualify basic conditions for being protect able under the copyright laws.

3. **Sui generis system of protection for Databases**

Sui generis protection of databases is largely guided by the European community. Directive on the legal protection of databases. The directive was passed by the European Parliament on 11 Mach 1996. A similar proposal, based on the bill (H.R.3531), was also introduced in the 104th United States Congress. The emerge focus is on the proposed WIPO treaty on intellectual property rights.

Copyright Protection Principles

The following are key principles concerning copyright protection:

- Copyright protects the manner of expression of information, not the idea or information itself.
- The work need not to be of very high quality for protection under the copyright. It only needs to be original.
- In principle it is the skill labor, and judgment of the author that is protected under the copyright laws irrespective of the form in which the product appears.
- The copyright in literary, dramatic, musical and artistic works belongs to the author of the work.
- The author has to be a person and not a corporation.

- In case, a work is produced with the aid of or is generated by computer, the person who undertakes the arrangements necessary for the creation of the work is considered as the author.
- In case, a work is produced by someone in the course of his employment, then the normal rule is that the copyright is owned by employers. Copyright will belong to the employer only if it is part of the employer duties to produce the work.
- No formalities such as registration or request to protect a work under copyright. The copyright notice need to appear on any work.
- The copyright owner can give a license to the work by others. Any assignment of copyright is to be in writing.
- Copying or making adaptations, of a works verbatim reproduction of a substantial part it done without the permission of copyright owner, is a breach of copyright.
- Use of copyright works for the purpose research and private study is generated permissible. There is no requirement sufficient acknowledgment.

Copyright act in India

The Indian Copyright Act 1957 was amended in 1994 to extend more effective protection to computer programs as literary works and for the protection of computer generated works. The meaning of literary work included works such as computer programs, tables and compilations including databases.

The meaning of Publication included making a work available to the public by issuing copies or by communicating the work to the public. The act provides for certain exemptions which do not constitute an infringement of copyright. For example, a fair dealing with a literary work (not being a computer programme) for the purposes of private use and search and preparations of criticism or review.

Purposes of teaching, research or scholarship include

(i) purposes of instructional activity at all levels in educational institutions including schools, colleges, universities and tutorial institution,

(ii) purposes of all other types of organized educational activity.

Purposes of research does not include purposes of industrial research, or purposes of research by bodies corporate, or purposes of research by bodies corporate (not being bodies corporate owned or controlled by government) or other association or body of persons for commercial purposes.

Databases of abstract and published articles

Lot of debate has ensued whether a database of abstracts infringes copyright of original authors. In this case, two questions are asked:

i. Do the abstracts simply report facts?

ii. Do the abstracts act as substitutes for the original texts?

In case of (i) there is no copyright in a fact or set of facts. If, on the other hand, the original item included some lengthy text, which is faithfully reproduced in the abstract, then it is likely to be considered a copyright infringement. The abstract should be significantly shorter than the original text, and should not act as a substitute for it.

Copyright law on multimedia

The copyright on multimedia are more complex than those for data bases. Because it deals with still pictures, moving images, voice, and music, besides electronic text, graphics, animations, etc. There is no doubt that multimedia has been considered as a standard facility. It is still not clear as to where the multimedia market will lie, other than in the home consumer market and education/training. The multimedia industry is littered with enough false starts for expression of caution. In spite of all these, there is no guarantee that multimedia can be expected to be a major player in information delivery in the next few years.

There are many issues such as the following which the publishers of multimedia must address.

I. **The right holder:** It is not necessarily as easy to identify who owns the rights to a particular performance of a piece of music or a small clip of a film. Considerable time can be spent hunting down the owner. The issue can not be ignored.

II. **Technologies to be used:** If it is necessary to provide rights to multimedia exploitation, it is important to define technologies correctly. It is unlikely that the rights owner will agree to broad nonspecific rights to all multimedia, so the definitions must be precise, and yet capable of flexibility. If it is necessary to a sound recording on CDTV, is it important to provide rights to explain on CD audio?.

III. **Geographical definition:** In the film business, restricting exploitation rights to a particular geographic area is not uncommon, it may be found that this sort of limitation is imposed on the publisher of a multimedia as well.

IV. **Language:** Multimedia products frequently offer multilingual choices to their users. It is essential to ensure that the rights on licenses include translation rights.

V. **Duration :** Because of the rapid development of multimedia, many rights holders are cautious about offering rights for more than a limited period: they want to see how this interesting marked develops and whether or not they can explain it yet further. One way around this would be for the publisher and rights owner to agree that if royalties reach a certain level in a certain period, then the license agreements is automatically renewed.

Conclusion

The central question for database industry is the prevention of outright piracy or illegal commercially significant use of the database. The lawa for database protection would require a sufficient degree of certainty in their application to be effective in supporting the commercial activity. Equally important are the needs for scientific and technological enterprise for free exchange of information and that data and informationin the anced by any legal treaty or instrument for proctection of databases.

References

1. Gautam. J.N. & Prodhani M.A. Copyright Status of Data Bases and Multimedia, Library Herald, Vol. 35. No. 1-2, April-September 1997, p.p 31-35
2. Gupta V.K. Copyright Issues Relating to Database Use, Desidoc Bulletin of Information Technology, Vol.17. No.4, July 1997, pp. 11-16.
3. Oppenhem, C, & Eisenschitz. T.S. Legal issues for Information Professionals Encyclopedia of Library and Information Science, 1994; 1994; v 54, Ed by Allent Kent and CM Hall, New York, Marcel Dekkar, pp. 224-261

9

Redefining IPR in The New Digital Environment: Some Concepts For College Libraries

Chitrarekha Kuffalikar

The information tide that is sweeping the rest of the world is rapidly approaching India. Internet connectivity is available in a variety of different forms ranging from low cost dial up network to large Internet service providers. Consumer Service is one of the major driving forces in various Information Centers. University and college libraries specially, professional libraries are on the forefront IPR in the digital age is acquiring an inseparable status and there is an urgent need to study the laws relating to these. If the college libraries have to really enjoy all the recent technologies in the true sense, they have to understand the concept of right to Information and their legalities in the right perspectives.

Internet & Content Generation

'Internet' which is simply defined as "network or networks connected to each other by telephone lines or cable has opened new vistas of knowledge converting the entire world into a global village. According to 'UNESCO' approximately 8,50,000 items (risen up) which includes books, journals, electronic and multimedia resources are published World Wide every year. Content generation at various levels using WWW (World Wide Web) has remarkably speeded up the connectivity. Strategic vision and adequate knowledge of the basic tools to develop contents are making institutions and countries more and more competitive". The generation of knowledge and information through local participation is another key area for getting the best out of connectivity. Knowledge economy and information capitalization underline the new information driven economy and business, at global level. Content creation involves 'collecting the information in various formats (text, graphics, sounds etc.) digitizing the information, organizing it using Web tools, storing, updating and providing access. Individuals need skills and tools to locate the communication pathways, information and audiences in a timely fashion in an appropriate format. Unequal access of communication leads to unequal advantages and ultimately to inequalities in social and economic opportunities.

Changing role of Libraries and Librarians

The librarians have to assume greater responsibilities in this 'Information age'. They have to concentrate on the managerial role, marketing their libraries and information products and act as negotiator to transfer the information as well as the technology to their clients. The other skills needed would also include interpersonal skills, planning skills and above all the IT skills.

The IT has made it impossible for the libraries vis-à-vis Information Centers to be self reliant in terms of collection and other aspects irrespective of their type and size. 'Dougherty and Hughes' (1991) have rightly identified that, "libraries and library services are no longer individual university problems and that, a collective approach is now absolutely essential".

The environment of the libraries becoming more IT oriented as it is a dynamic resource for global sharing as the cost of information' is minimum and source does not get exhausted even with unlimited use.

Right to Information

The concern over human rights has acquired new dimensions in recent times. The idea of unrestricted flow of information between nations began to crystallize in US. First, the American Society of Newspaper Editors adopted a resolution urging the political parties to support "freedom of information" & unrestricted flow of information throughout the world. A number of conferences discussed the above issues in Brussels (1948), Berne (1952), Paris (1971) and Rome (1992). Subsequently the free flow ideology became an integral part of the US political ideology and foreign policy. The UN General Assembly resolution-59.1 issued in 1946 made the first reference to 'Free flow of information' later known as Freedom of Information Act (FIA) 1966 was enacted with certain conditions in Finland (1951), Sweeden (1966), France (1978), Australia (1982), Newzealand (1982), Canada (1983) and USA (1996). The Indian constitution does not provide this right though, it is only an implied right from other rights. This notion first appeared in 1989 when Hon. Shri V.P.Singh announced the increase in access to Information which was thoroughly examined by a 'Special Task force'. He rightly pointed out that right to Information will be enshrined in our constitution. The Right to Information bill drafted by Press Council of India (1996), Freedom of Information bill (1997) of H.D.Shourie, Prasar Bharati bill is also worth mentioning here. A number of States took initiative in this regard like Karnataka (Freedom of Press Bill 1983), Tamil Nadu, Goa, Madhya Pradesh, Rajasthan (Freedom of Information Bill 1997) etc.

Copyright

'Copyright' is basically the right to copy and make use of literary, dramatic, musical and artistic works, cinematographic films and records and to broadcast. Copyright is a proprietary right and comes into effect as soon as the work is created. It is the right generally secured by law to others of literary, dramatic and artistic works to authorize production or reproduction of such works. Article 27 of "Universal Declaration of Human Rights" adopted by "General Assembly of UN on December 10th, 1948" states 'A copyright also provides certain exemptions to enable the reproduction of work for public interest'. The first national copyright law enacted in England in 1709 also known as the "Statue of Anne" gave exclusive rights to authors to print or authorize the printing of their works. The acts slowly broadened in scope though the word "copy-right" remained the same. Subsequently, the French Copyright act "droit de autheur" (author's right) came into existence which is far more appropriate extending this right to other creative like artists, musicians, painters, choreographers and a host of other creators.

In the year 1911 the copyright of England was passed in India, further revised in 1914, the first copyright of India was passed and revised comprehensively in 1957. The act was amended again between 1982 to 1994. The basic reason for this being effective copyright protection promotes and rewards human creativity and support for intellectual, cultural and economic activity.

Intellectual Property Rights

Padma V. Upadhyaya has defined "IPR as the creation of human mind. A human beings potential efforts lead to intellectual outcomes, which in turn have considerable value in economy. Rights associated with Intellectual Property which gives legal protection is referred to as Intellectual property rights or (IPR)".

The World Trade Organization (WTO) is a successor to General Agreement on Tariffs and Trade 1994 (GATT) a permanent World Trade body. IPRs which comes under the ambit of GATT is a collective term which includes several independent IPRs namely patents, copyright, trademark, Industrial design, geographical indications and protection of undisclosed information. The "World Intellectual Property Organization (WIPO)" has been actively involved in this venture and is responsible for administering 'Berne Copyright Convention (1996) which has proposed several changes but two are of particular significance to Information professionals i.e. legal issues of concern to library and Information Sector (LISLEX).

A copyright generated in a member country of the "Berne Convention" is automatically protected in all member countries without any need for registration however, the rights will not be automatically available in countries that are not members of 'Berne Convention'. The IPRs are mainly for the benefit of creators of work, inventions and designs. These rights are granted for a limited period except for trademark where the protection period could be extended by renewals. India is a signatory to 'Berne Convention' and has a very good copyright legislation compared to other countries. Copyright protection extends to expression of an idea which should be in a tangible form to get protection. Merely sounds and gestures cannot be copyrighted. Hence, any information transmitted in 'Internet' is a subject matter of copyright.

IPR in the Digital Age

In the sweeping digital environment all over the world, the owners of the copyright of the intellectual works are confronted and exploited by a variety of technological innovations. Computer programmes and databases are also considered literary works and hence are protected by copyright even in India. The emergence of Information super highway in the recent years has wider implications on the protection and dissemination of Intellectual works. The effect of digital technology warrants revision and updating of existing copyright laws to safeguard the interests of copyright owners as the digitization of information has forced the violation of copyright in leaps and bounds. The main issues concern today are, security of data, fair use, appropriate long term preservation measures availability of digital publications etc.

'Murry Gell Hann' has rightly revealed that, "the information explosion about which so much has been said and written is to a great extent an explosion of misinformation". The digital revolution has made the problems more acute and hence, consideration of IPR has become more crucial and timely. 'Internet' has posed many questions and hence it has become mandatory to protect commercial interests of creators work. As the information available on 'Internet' is in public domain it is extremely important to make the digital resources as reliable as possible. Several efforts are being made to improve the authenticity of digital data, to make the global digital scenario more reliable.

Global View

"Dr. Tamara Eisenschitze" (1993) in his article 'EC Draft directive on legal protection of databases ;- an information scientists reaction (published in the series of LISLEX Column) has spoken in detail about the use of databases by Information Scientists and UK copyright law. Compulsory licensing , unfair extraction and utilization, infringements etc. In the same series "Sorah Ellis" and "Charles Oppenheim" (1993) have spelt out their views regarding "Data protection and the media" in the light of "Data Protection Act 1984" and European Conventions (EC) draft directives, protection, privacy and the media, EC draft directive and the media, media libraries and Information Centers etc. Part IV of the same series by the above authors speaks about the "Data Protection amongst UK media librarians". It is a survey carried among large number of UK media librarians and Information Scientists and a few UK Journalists to identity their attitudes towards 8DPA and the EC draft. The paper concludes that, the Draft will impose intolerable burdens on information science community, specially, in Media and has recommended the librarians to undertake data protection awareness campaign for its members.

Another very major issue of concern in the present digital environment is the "Communication Decency Act" (CDA).

IPR ISSUES FOR LIBRARY & INFORMATION SCIENCE PROFESSIONALS IN INDIA

The content creating agencies and the IP right holders attribute 'Internet' as one of the biggest copying machine and demand the measurement of each drop of knowledge being put in the 'cyberspace'. The issues are of extreme concern to all the libraries specially the professional Information Centers. They are mainly because;

- Digital data is easy to capture, store, process and download.
- It is just impossible to keep a track of the copyright infringement in the digital environment, because of the facilities like structuring, restructuring, mixing and remixing of information with the sound waves etc.

In the present Internet environment where, more and more universities and colleges are computerizing their operations and services, it is time to ponder over questions as;

a) Is the website copyrightable in terms of content, the source code, layout etc.

b) Is linking and downloading from websites legal / illegal?

c) Viability of new invention, ID and password etc.

The economic value of copyright is also of great concern to us. We have to therefore, visualize the issues which are relevant in view of the rights provided to a person who owns the intellectual rights. The mandatory obligation is a must for library professionals to perform challenging services in this IT dominated Information Society. Reproduction by the libraries, commercial photocopying and fair use are some of the issues to be dealt with great care in recent times. The emergence of mobile consumers (M-commerce) with the existing problems opened windows for the digital criminals which have to be handled very carefully. Hence It has become imperative that, with Internet and E-commerce, institutions, must familiarize themselves with the scope of IPR that could be implemented in their website .

The Strategic Information Technology (SCIT) Plan of 15th June 1999 is also serving as a guide to the member states from 2000 onwards. It has defined the "Minimum Modernization Standards (MMS)". WIPO has become a well defined project in the 21st century, whose role as a facilitator for providing details on technologies and related standards in materialization of IPR is worth mentioning. The IT act 2000 of India is also a welcome move as its main objective being, legal recognition for transactions carried out by means of Electronic data interchange.

IPR issues for College Libraries

The modern IT clubbed with the 'Internet' has opened new gateways for libraries to disseminate knowledge. Among all sound resource full libraries like professional college libraries are in the forefront adopting these technologies. In order to manage these vast resources efficiently, Library & Information Science Professionals (LISP) are being trained. Funding bodies like UGC etc., & parent organizations are becoming more and more professional to get the best possible services for their clients.

In almost all the colleges, 'Internet' is largely being used as a tool for Acquisition, Technical Processing, Retrospective Conversion and to provide various Information Services such as Referral Service, OPAC, CAS, content services, SDI and allied services including reference services, by resource sharing. The student community is the largest beneficiary as they are the constant users of the 'Net'. Thus, IPR is of great concern to all such libraries. The points discussed so far in this article are concerned to college libraries also. Is the net, really being utilized for Academic purposes? is a question worth mentioning and to be thought about seriously.

'Satarkar'(2001) in his article has clearly identified the problems regarding the information services of the academic libraries in the light of the fundamental laws of library science. He has clearly stated that, 'Though the basic existence of these libraries rests on the five fundamental laws, one should always bear in mind to strictly abide by the IPR while providing Information Services to their beneficiaries.

Evaluation of Internet Resources

Hence, in the above context 'Karabi Basu' (1999) feels that, it would be extremely vital to 'evaluate the Internet' resources with the help of IPR guidelines before providing these services to its beneficiaries. The criteria for evaluation as suggested may be (1) Authority - regarding the authenticity of author, (2) Accessibility, (3) Arrangement, (4) Currency, (5) Response time, (6) Stability, (7) Accuracy, (8) Target group, (9) Coverage, (10) Completeness Style, format etc.

Divyanand & Lalita Koti (1999) in their article have also suggested a number of criteria for evaluating the Internet resources. These include a) Content, b) Creditability, c) Critical thinking, d) copyright, e) citations, f) continuity, g) censorship, h) connectivity, I) Comparability, j) context etc.

Conclusion

At the outset IPR in digital age is acquiring an inseparable status and there is an urgent need to study the laws related to printing and other media at different levels. If one has to make best use of all the media available, one has to surely learn, monitor and incorporate new developments, participate in consortiums related to digital media, continually update and validate digital content by coordinating with legal representatives and adopt appropriate strategies to limit risk factors.

The 21st century Libraries vis-à-vis Information Centers & the professionals find themselves at the threshold of an explosive revolution.

The developments in communication technology have triggered unprecedented changes in corporate activities. The purpose of 'Internet' is to make its content economically viable for the benefit of the newly emerging information society. This would largely depend on how successfully one is able to resolve the issues related to IPR.

If the college libraries have to really enjoy all the recent technologies in the true sense and to give all the necessary care and delight to their beneficiaries, they have to positively understand the concept of 'right to Information' and their legalities in the true sense.

References

1. Adam, Lishan (1997): Content and the Web for African development, J. of Inf. Sc. 23 (1) ,; pp. 91 - 97.
2. Ashok Babu, T (1998): Right to Information. IASLIC Seminar vol. xviii; pp 21- 26.
3. Basu, Karabi (1999): Evaluation of Internet resources CALIBER Seminar Vol. VI (18-20 Feb); pp 296 - 301.
4. Bomanwar, V.J.(1998) : Indian Copyright act and Intellectual property. IASLIC Seminar vol. xviii ; pp. 47 - 51.
5. Cawkell, Tony (1997) :The information superhighway : a review of some determining factors. J of Inf.Sc, 23 (3); pp. 187 - 208.
6. Choudhary (P.K.) :Intellectual property Rights: Issue and concerns. NACLIN.et al (2000) 22nd-25th IIT Chennai ; pp. 275 - 286.
7. Datta, Subrata (1998) :Application of copyright & right to Information act in the areas of Inf. Technology. IASLIC Seminar vol.xviii. ; pp. 27-31.

8. Divyanand, K & : (1999) : India's educational threshold of 21st century. pp. 85-99.

9. E.isenschitz, Tamara :The EC draft directive on the legal protection of databases : An (1993) Information Scientist's reaction. Jr. of Inf. Sc. 19 pp. 77-80.

10. Ellis, Sarah & : Data protection & the media-background to the DPA 1984 & Oppenheim, Charles (1993) EC draft directive on data protection. Ibid; pp. 85 - 97.

11. Ellis, Sarah: Attitudes to data protection among UK Librarians. Ibid.; Oppenheim, Charles (1993) pp 99 - 117.

12. Gupta, V.K. : IPR Information : Analysis and drafting of patent claims for Pongannaya, N.B. R&D Scientists. J. Intellectual Property rights. 4(6) ; (1999) pp 325 - 38.

13. Iyengar (Sreenidhi) (1996) : Library Standards - Anmol Publications Ltd., New Delhi.

14. Kaul (M.K.) (2000) : Networking knowledge : The role of libraries. NACLIN. 22nd - 25th IIT Chennai.; pp 219 - 230.

15. Kuffalikar, C.K.(2001) : Managing Information in the digital age : Some IPR issues for college libraries . NUCLA. Conference Vol. (18th Feb) ; pp- 105 - 110.

16. Mashelkar (R.A.) (2000) : The Role of WIPONET in the development and transfer of technology and its contribution to modernization of Intellectual property service. Information Today and Tomorrow, 19(2); pp 2 - 6.

17. Mc Murdo, George (1997):Cyber porn & Communication decency. J. Of Inf. Sc.23(i); pp 81 - 90.

18. Ramaiah, L.S.(1998): Right to InformationIASLIC Seminar v.xviii ; pp21-26.

19. Ramesh Babu, B & Kasirao,V.(1998): Information access & copyright; pp53-55.

20. Saha, R. (2000) : Intellectual Property rights & internet. DESICOC bulletin of Inf. Technology, 20(1-2);pp13-19.

21. Satarkar,S. P. (2001) :' Swamitma Kayada ani Granthalaye', Dnyangangotri,Yashawatrao Chavan Open University,Nasik, 1(3); pp 25-32

22. Singh (Sonal) (2000) : Internet & the role of Libraries. Journal of Library and Information Sc. 25(1) ; pp 27-37.

23. Tripathi, T. (1998) : Access to Information : issues relating to developing countries. IASLIC Seminar Vol.XVIII ; pp 7-11.

24. Upadhyay (Padma) (2000) : Intellectual property rights in the digital age. NACLIN 22nd- 25th IIT Chennai.; pp260-266.

25. Vijayraghavan, M.S. (2000) : Information Technology : A force multiplier estraordinary. DESIDOC bulletin of Inf.Technology;20(1-2); pp21-27.

26. Yadava (R.S.) (2000) : IPR in the digital WTO era with special reference to Indian Systems of medicine. Potentialities and pitgalls. NACLIN 22nd-25th IIT Chennai.; pp 267-274.

10

Convergences In "Knowledge Society" Aspects Of Copyright Law And Cybernetics

Bhavani Prasad Panda
Minati Panda
Bharat B. Das

India is well placed at the dawn of the knowledge era. Over the ages the great Indian thinkers have taken an integrated view of life as a fusion of mind, body and intellect. Their vision of knowledge is unique and reflects in the rich heritage. The taskforce of the Planning Commission in India, steered by Dr. APJ Abdul Kalam recently submitted that the strategy for transformation of India as super power lies in appropriate tapping of all knowledge resources and makes use in the confluence of civilization and the emerging technological streams.

Taking the inspiration from the Report, which visualizes that "Knowledge Society" (hereinafter KS) is the imperative agenda to meet all future challenges both locally and globally. The essential feature of the KS is:

1. It uses knowledge through all its constituents and endeavors to empower and enrich its people.
2. It uses knowledge as a powerful tool to drive societal transformation.
3. It is learning society committed to innovation.
4. It has the capacity to generate, absorb, disseminate and protect knowledge and also use it to create economic wealth and social good for all its constituents.

5. It enlightens its people to take an integrated view of life as a fusion of mind, body and spirit.

The motive force in the impeding KS essentially are – first, the transformation for a just and equitable society, secondly, wealth generation and thirdly, protection of knowledge. The purpose of the paper is to make an attempt to reflect the prevailing knowledge protection in terms of Copyright and consider the necessary adaptations to KS with reference to cyber networking.

There is an imminent need to design and implement an effective Intellectual Property Rights (hereinafter IPR) system to safeguard the interests of KS. In this pursuit, it is essential to do value addition to generate IPR in these areas, preserve and invest for a rich harvest later, rather than throwing off for low cost service benefits immediately. The creator and possessor of knowledge need be assured with institutional support system. The information technology diluted the geographic limitations and advancing ahead to match to the speed of time, the process of globalization is threatening the appropriation of elements of collective knowledge for the commercial benefit of few. In the power politics, the twin objectives for a nation state are essentially economic prosperity coupled with national security. The advancements of information technology will not only compel us to a review the legal and practical meaning of the notions of individual privacy, but also that of the privacy of nations. Still more the developments of very economic, multiple and worldwide network for communicating information much speedier is likely to shift power from the government monopoly to private and individual performers. While IT will vastly increase the capacity of a government to monitor its subjects, the governmental hegemony over the information distribution will sharply decline. The form of public opinion generated by the civil society players independent of ministerial inputs will influence the finality of decisions. This will mean that greater attention will have to be provided to the quality, clarity and reliability of information disseminated. Accountability and authenticity of the information/knowledge need be confirmed and effectively secured.

The composition bandwidth has in fast been doubling every

year, thus reducing the gap between time and distance, and enabling information available at any time and at any space. Through different tools in IT, information gets stored in a digital form as bits and bytes and gets multiplied then these bits traverse in the network. In essence the connected information creates information base that has different tools in IT, information gets stored in a digital form as bits and bytes and gets multiplied then these bits traverse in the network. In essence the connected information creates information base that has the potential for a chain reaction and ignites a knowledge explosion. This can mean prosperity if that knowledge power can be chanalised and sublimed into wealth. Knowledge is always not been a public/ common property, but it is, of course recognized, to a certain extent as private property and capable of ownership by private person. With changing times "Knowledge" is gaining the significance of pure and simple economic index. Thus when the development gauge uses 'knowledge' in terms of economic scale, the protection dimensions for the sublimation technology of knowledge assumes a predominant value. The IPR regime is attempting to take charge and to harmes "the knowledge" and the concomitant econometrics thereof. Convergence of geography coupled with the advantages brought by IT puts all the stakeholders of knowledge society (knowledge workers, knowledge industry, knowledge consumers and knowledge merchandise") on heels. The concern obviously is the security of the "knowledge merchandise", its protection and equitable share return from the investment made on "knowledge market". The focus is, therefore, on the protection of "knowledge economy", and dissemination and distribution, of rates and values.

Dmitri Sklyarov Case: In July 2001, Mr. Dmitri Sklyarov (27), the Russian Programmer was arrested amid high drama in America, just after he delivered an invited talk at "Defcon", an international computer conference held in Las Vegas. The arrest was based on a complaint by the US software company Adobe Systems that a product developed by "ElcomSoft", his employer back in Russia, violated the copyright of their software for e-books (Electronic version of popular books). The software, developed by Mr. Dmitri Sklyarov, enabled users to break the encryption of Adobe's e-book software and make back-up copies of the sofware or uses it on other devices such as hand-held computers. Such software tools are not illegal in Russia; indeed back-up features are mandatory. Because of Internet they would be easily accessed in America. Adobe invoked the Digital Millennium Copyright Act 1998, the US Government decided to make it a test case of this cyber-age statute. The Russian computer whiz kid, though enlarged on bail was restrained from returning to his home-land and faced five years of imprisonment in US prisons and a half million dollar fine. In the face of outraged protests by the global IT community and threats that all Adobe products would be boycotted, the complainant company withdrew its suit, but the case was persecuted by governmental prosecutors.

On 14th December, 2001, the US District Court in San Jose freed Mr. Dmitri Sklyarov five months after his dramatic arrest in the first ever case, testing the limits of new cyber laws, however, he is required give depositions in the case for both sides if required - the US Government and his parent company. This means the focus shifts to the company. India needs to consider these intricacies in its IT policy and provide appropriately in the Convergence law.

A study by the Business Software Alliance (BSA) and software Publishers Association (SPA) reveals that for the years 1994-95 the losses to the industry amounted to $12.2 billions and $13.3 billions respectively. In many countries the quantity of pirated software exceeded the number of legitimate copies. In Vietnam, it was estimated that 99% of software was pirated, with the figures for China being 96%. Even in Western Europe, 86% of software in Greece was considered to be pirated, 51% in France, with the UK being the most law abiding country with a figure of 38%. For the US figure of software piracy was 26%.

Copyright and the cyber world

The thrust of this paper is to understand the dynamics of copyright protection law in the digital World Wide Web (www) in the emerging scenario. One debate that keeps the lawmakers engaged is the issue whether it is possible to comprehend a viable legal regime to police copyrighting in cyberspace. Cyberspace has emerged as a transcendental jurisdictional artifice paving way for superhighway for artificial intelligence and knowledge transmission and convergence. Internet services as good copying machine and information disseminator. For protecting a copyright there are three essential steps that need be fulfilled viz.

1. Whether a particular work is eligible for protection?
2. Whether there is scope for protection available for the work? And
3. Whether limitations on the scope of protection that may be allowed?

The Internet juxtaposes with concomitant problems at each of these above steps of copyright protection. Copyright protection and policing www is a difficult task if not impossible. Digital access to material involves copying of the original material and reproduction of it takes place in the following contexts:

1. When a work is entered into a computer (on disk, diskette, CD-ROM or other storage device) or into a RAM for more than a temporary period;
2. When a printed document is converted into a digital file(scanning);
3. When non-written works (e.g. Photographs, motion video and sound recordings) are converted into digital form;
4. When a digital file is transferred (uploaded) to a Bulletin Board System or other server;
5. When a digital file is transferred from one user on a network to another; and
6. When a user's computer is used to access a file residing on another computer.

In the cyber-net interface the copyright protection intervenes in the following situations,

1. creation of intellectual property itself;
2. when uploading the content;
3. while transmitting the content;
4. at the time of accessing the content; and
5. at the time of using the content.

First, a very radical group suggests "whether in this cyber regime, there should be copyright protection at all essential, when knowledge is disseminated for furthering and enriching it, and what protection right, when the work is uploaded by the author of the work himself? Is it not relinquishment of the right, by the very act of uploading the work ?; secondly, a group of moderators who suggest that the right of net-publishers may be effectively protected by a "sui generis" form of right, however, it is still an idea and shall take time for any crystallization into law; and thirdly, the conservationists argue for copyright protection with an effective policing regime ? Around the world, the nations are extending copyright to computer program. An analysis of the legal problems confronted in copyright and facilitation of internet to the knowledge world, will throw light on the issues need be concerned with, and may provide policy direction for regulating regime.

Infringement of a copyright will expose the perpetrator to a civil action brought by the copyright owner, but the law also provides of number of criminal offences which may be committed by those engaged in the protection or supply of infringing copies for commercial purposes. The act of copying in the context means "involving in the reproduction of the work, or a substantial part of the work in any material form. This is to include "storing the work in any medium by electronic means". For example, the use of some form of scanning device to transform text into electronic format will constitute an infringement of copyright. "From start to finish, copyright never stops anyone working on the same lines, upon the same sort of basic ideas, and copyright cannot be effective against anyone who produces something independently."

The Copyright law defines the words "computer program"

and "literary work". Reading the two definitions together it implies that a computer program recorded in any digital media including CD, floppy of any storage device is considered as a "literary work". The right over the same is a protected intellectual property. The peculiarity with the computer program is that it involves a series of instructions or commands issued to the hardware of the computer, which activates the artificial intelligence in the computer to perform the task in a particular manner. The software, as is being popularly called, is an intangible form of artificial intelligence creation, and has a definite and considerable property value. Because of the intangible nature of computer program, the traditional law of contract i.e. the law of ales of goods can not be brought into use. Considering the nature of creativity and the nature of usage by the world at large, including the creator of the software, it is most appropriate, to protect as a copyright, for the buyer/licensee is permitted only to copy the software ina limited way. Copyright protects the expressive aspects of creation, but functional attributes falls outside the scope, there has been suggestions that patent law could have protected the functional aspects of the software as is the case in some jurisdiction or a sui-generis protection could have been more appropriate. In the coming paragraph an effort will be made to look into the arguments against, the nature of protection to the computer program under copyright law.

Computer program is a part-expression, part –machine, part writing and part-invention/creation. It is only machine-readable. The copy of which is functionally identical to- and indistinguishable from- the original or copyright protected version. The copying is very easy, economical and can remain undetectable. The software has several components-commands and sequences and different variety of intellectual/innovative skills and the same result, there accrues a problem to protect the intellectual property right to the subsequent author. Much more complicated issue is whether the new program based on the earlier program can be protected by copyright law? May be the process patent over such innovation is more appropriate for the interest of the software industry cannot be ignored. Alternatively, the underlying commands/instructions in the software being intangible, and both the copyright law and the patent law not being completely affording to protect the intellectual property in the software, the embedded knowledge in the computer program need to be geared up for a new category of protection and administration.

In England and America, in a limited way the patentability of computer program is being considered appropriate. In UK, the judicial interpretations to the technical and mechanized aspects of software and similar content in the innovation, is being held to be the scope for patent protection, though the definition of software is specifically covered under the UK Copyright Act 1977. The reasoning appended for patent protection is that the better suits in protecting the "methods" and the "process" in a certain rather than the very creation as is being purported in the copyright law. The American Courts also held that the computer program could be granted patent protection, though initially the courts were reluctant to bring software into the ambit of the patent protection holding that computer program are copyrightable including the microcode, the operating systems and application as "literary work". However, the American approach to the protection of computer program is doubly insulated i.e. software industries avail copyright protection for the literary work and patent protection for the machine component of the computer program and the program are protected irrespective of its source code and/ or object code. On the issue of protection of intellectual property in computer software whether through the Patent or Copyright route, it should be a consideration more for protection well insulated rather than toying with the idea fitting the new developments into an existing legal regime not meant/thought over for such venture. The software industry is pumping more of its resource to provide new conveniences through the dream programmers.

In India, the right given to author or creator of works, such as books, films or even computer programs is recognized against copying or other exploitations. This right commences automatically with the creation of the work, when the creator is a "qualifying person" or the work has been published or broadcasted in an appropriate manner. The owner of the copyright in a work has the exclusive right to control publication, performance, broadcasting, and the making of adaptations of the work. The law supports with both civil comedies for recovering the damages as well as criminal prosecution against the copyright violators for infringements with a view to make commercial gain. To cope up with the demands of cyber networking, in 1984 bringing "computer program" with in the definition of "literary work" amended the copyright law. Again keeping in tune to the digital technology, in 1994 the copyright law incorporated and included "reproduction right of literary, dramatic or musical work includes storing of it in any medium by electronic means".

The new definition of cinematograph film and sound recordings include recording of the audio and visuals in any medium, which includes digital medium as well as. In this background, it is seen that a software package is a complex collection of separate rights, it includes computer program, which causes a computer to process information. However, databases are included in the definition of literary work, but as for as copyright is concerned it is necessary to distinguish between the right subsisting as a table or compilation and copyright on the underlying works. Copyright can subsist in a literary work consisting of a "compute program tables and compilation including databases" quite independently from the copyright, which may be subsisting, in any work comprised in the building of database. There prevails a distinction between "computer generated" and "computer assisted" (computer aided) works, the former has copyright but not without problems of copyrighting but the later do not fall with in the scope of special treatment by law. The difficulties of copyright in "computer generated work" are with regard to

(i) That a number of competing individuals may claim to have made the arrangement necessary for the creation of the work,

(ii) Would the author of the underlying software have the claim to copyright in the output?

(iii) Would two or more identical works produced by different individuals using the same program generate all quality for protection as original literary work?

Substantial similarity in copyright works; Infringement of copyright does not require that an exact copy be made of the whole of work. Copying of a substantial portion will suffice however there lies subtle difficulty in identification of what may be regarded as a substantial portion not only in quantitative terms but also in qualitative terms. In addressing the issue, the courts have focused the economic consequences of the activity. If the portion copied can be regarded as constituting a significant portion of the work's value to the copyright owner, infringement may be found even though it constitutes a relatively small portion of the whole. In the case of computer program, the novelty and value may lie in one routine which constitutes a comparatively small portion of what is otherwise a fairly standard program, and copying of this would amount to an infringement of copyright. It is not the issue in substantial similarity matters whether 9,999 out of 10,000 characters copied or it is only a mere copy of the 100 of 10,000 characters.

Literal and non-literal copying

In the case of computer program, claims of copyright infringement fall into two categories. The first, and considerably the simpler, concerns the situation where there is evidence of similarity at the level of the code and comes under the heading of literal copying. At the most blatant level this will constitute what is frequently referred to as "software piracy" where illicit copies of software packages are made with a view to being distributed and sold.

In IBCOS Computers Ltd. V. Barclays Mercantile Finance Ltd., the first defendant had been employed by the plaintiff on the development of a software product intended for use of the agriculture dealers which was marketed under the name ADS. On leaving its employment, he developed a further a competing product, which was marketed .under the name of Unicorn. The plaintiff alleged that sufficient features of this were copied from the original to constitute an infringement of copyright. In determining the question whether infringement had occurred, Jacob, J held that the court should determine whether there was a sufficient degree work, would establish an inference of copying. The onus swifts on to defendant to establish, that the similarities were explicable by causes other than copying. Evidence that "functional necessity" served to narrow the range of options open to the defendant.

It is the resemblances in essentials, the small, redundant, even mistaken elements of the copyright work, which carry the greatest weight. This is because they are the least likely to have been the result of independent design. Billofer Mashcinenfabrik gmbH v. TH Dixon & Co.Ltd. provided the precedent that trivial items may well explicit the most expressive testimony. Evidence was presented that the same words erroneously spelt in the same bit of code, which served no useful purpose for the functioning of the program. The court held that in respect of one element of the program there are as many as 22 identical variable, 8 identical labels, 1 identical remark, 31 identical code line and 1 identical redundant variable. That is plainly copying and enough in itself to constitute a significant part. Although the ADS and Unicorn programs have different visual effects, it was held that the defendant had taken "shortcuts by starting with ADS and making considerable additions and modifications.

Justifiable similarities

In any copyright litigation, it will be an issue relating to fact whether a later work has been copied from an earlier, identification may not be a simple task as the question seems to be, for the civil suits the standard of proof refers to preponderance of probabilities. That a party responsible for the production of an exact copy of a work could establish that this was entirely serendipitous, the task of determining the issue will be more complex in the event that the later version is not an exact copy of the original. In computer program, a variety of producers may be operating in the same field, in such situation, and especially given the identical constraints which may operate, close similarities between two works may occur in the absence of deliberate copying or plagiarism, commonness in alma-matter may also result in the production of substantially similar programs.

An independent creator has nothing to fear from the law of copyright. Where work is conducted on behalf of a third party the nature and extent of instruction given will be significant in determining whether an infringement occurred or not. The competing software firms use the so called "clean-room" technique, i.e. ensures that employers responsible for the design of components which are likely to be similar to those of others are kept deliberately ignorance of the earlier work.

"Fair-dealing" is a statutorily provided in exception; it permits for copying of a protected work for the purpose research and private study. The range of the defiance extends to critiquing, commenting, news-reporting and teaching, scholarship and related academic usage. Fair use exempts license from the copyright owner. Fair dealing allows a degree of copying without infringement of the copyrighted work, but the supplementary question, how much? can not be categorically answered, it is always a question of fact, and the courts will look into the purpose and character of the use. There are certain difficulties in the cybernetics, the first, though the researcher may be requiring only a small portion of the work but copying in small parts/portions is a difficult task in software copyright protected work compared to the copying of the whole text of the program and secondly, the digital copying is a fragile creature and in a research conducted to its makeup can dodge the user with terminal damage or total corrupt intervention, which usually happens very easily for various reasons. It has been usual practice, as a safeguard measure to preserve a second / backup copy, and this is considered as reasonable in fair dealing. However, de-compilation / encrypting of a program will be ultra-virus to the fair use defence and infringe the protection law. As soon as the research ends the status of the "copy" made will change.

Reverse engineering in software is the most controversial issue. Computer programs are broadly of two categories –operating system and application program. Generally the producer of the operating system provides the functional manual of the system; however, when it is not available reverse engineering is the technique attempted. This may as well happen with application program. The sheer object of such de -compilation is to discover information about the user interface of an application package, which may then be used as the basis for the attempt to produce a substantially similar package. Most often in such cases the defence is "that the Internet was to reproduce the "look and feel" of the original package.

Software copyright infringing incidences

The owner of the copyright in a work has the right to determine whether copies of that work might be made available to the public. The acts of performing or showing the protected work in public are reserved to the copyright owner. Making of adaptation of a protected work i.e. an infringement of altered version of the program or a translation of it will impact on copyright protection. In the eventuality of an infringement being reported, the courts are empowered to grant the following relief:

1. Temporary and permanent injunctions;
2. Impounding and destruction of all infringing copies, including master copies;
3. Actual monetary damages plus the infringer's profits;
4. Statutory damages;
5. Litigation costs and reasonable attorney's fees.

'Anton Piller action order : Anton Piller order allows a Local Commissioner, appointed by the court and sometimes accompanied by the Copyright owners' representatives, to enter the premises of the suspected counterfeiter and assist in identifying the infringing good. An Anton Piller order can authorize the Commissioner to seek police assistance, break locks or set up decoy purchases. The Commissioner is the "eyes and ears" of the court, so to speak. This has dramatically improved results as the infdringers quickly come forward to settle the case with the copyright-owner. A recent example of the enforcement of the Anton Pillar order is against two popular Computer Training Centers in New Delhi, at the instance of NASSCOM and BSA. The litigation was settled with in 10 weeks, which included the payment of damages to the BSA and an agreement to realize all software used at the centers. The offender institutions also provided an undertaking that they would not in future use, copy, sell. Offer for sale or deal illegally in any software of the complaints" members.

Moral Rights: First, an author has the right to be identified as such in every copy of the work which is issued to the public; second right is the converse of the above referring to false attribution of the work. This right extends to all works including computer programs and to work carried out in the course of employment; and thirdly, an author has the right to object to any derogatory treatment of the work. The right extends in respect of any "addition to, deletion from or alteration to, or adaptation of the work which amount to distortion or mutilation of the work or is otherwise prejudicial to the honor of reputation of the author or director.

Copyright protection and Internet services

Between the creator (owner) of the copyright and the end-user (consumer) there are lot of intermediaries who assist in facilitating both the initiator and knowledge user. The intermediaries in the cyber paradigm are Internet Service Providers (ISPs hereinafter), they comprise: information providers access providers, network providers and other related utility providers. It is unlikely that a single legal entity provides all the complete range of services. Quite many of these ISPs provide the service free of relatively free and hence their position in the context of copyright infringement is not clear. Implicitly the network providers would be infringing copyright whenever they transmitted information/knowledge protected under the copyright law (facilities by placing copyrighted material on the internet without the authorization of the owner of the work) is said to have

i. Infringed the copyright in t he information/knowledge by making a copy of the work, and

ii. To be also liable for impliedly authorizing others to take copies as a person.

ISPs though are service providers, tantamount to tread into the forbidden boundaries of copyright causing serious damage to the owner of the right. The liability accrues more from the fact they tacitly assist, aid, or instigate by impliedly extending the authorization of the right which they themselves do not possess, and further more, they do not have any control over the end user. The issues those crop up when a subscriber maker's copyright owners are - if that person is liable for any infringement copies made by persons downloading the material? If the ISP responsible as a facilitator by authorizing infringement? There are difficulties in identifying who and where is the person who made the infringed material available through the Internet. By the process of "catching" that is, copying the material on the user's PC to speed up future access to a website, materials are generally downloaded during the transmission en route the Internet, the material traverses through several operators in several jurisdictions. This means the copyrighted material passes unauthorized through several hands and most of the facilitators may not even know what message transmitted through their facility. Subject to express or implied licenses, network operators, would be infringing copyright whenever they transmitted a message protect by the copyright, whether or not the message infringed copyright when it left the sender. The position of the service providers is not altogether clear in the context of copyright infringement. The infringement can occur at any of three interfaces viz.

1. at the originator level, by uploading the material which he / she is not entitled to;
2. by the intermediaries ISPs for facilitating the originators and the end users to access to the protected material without having any control over the illegal beneficiaries,
3. the end user, by accessing to the copyright protected material by the "process of catching".

Both reproduction and communication to public rights are

now extended to substantially all kinds of works in digital format, the Copyright Act, 1957 has not specifically defined storage and it is a matter of interpretation to determine whether temporary and permanent reproduction will form part of this right.

The shift from "wheels revolution" to the "information technology revolution" has elements of uncertainty, challenging and interesting times. Attempt to apply yesterday's concepts of tomorrow's society appears to the futile. A few aspects of life will survive the cybernetics unscathed bu this is itself a natural process that is set in. The parameters of e-commerce set by the IT Act, 2000 stands more on four key cornerstones of trustworthy transactions – integrity, authenticity, confidentiality and non-repudiation, where the certification agencies will issue certificates to individuals, corporate and business entries. The IT Act, 2000 is wide enough to protect the rights of the web-page owner. An uploaded material in the net satisfies the requirement of data under the IT Act. 2000 Section 2 (o), which means "whoever downloads, copies or extracts any data or database" or reduces the value of data shall be liable to pay damage under section 43 of IT Act and also liable for hacking under section 65 of the same act. This is at the moment an extreme proposition and interpretation, but the changing times with market economy and many more erstwhile copyright aspects will find IT Act type damages, which of course is not the real intent of the IT Act, 2000.

In India, the copyright law is governing the computer software generally. The Copyright Act 1957 is being described as one of the stringent protection law in the world. The layering process, as well as, the opportunity for such advocacy for intellectual property is just beginning. The validation of the existing copyright law and expansions made to encompass software protection appears as a mere cosmetic approach. Every time a consumer buys a computer loaded with unlicensed software, or buys unlicensed software products he is party to the crime. The menace of software piracy or violation of Copyright affects not only the potential of software development in India but also our country's economy, besides sending negative signals to potential investors. The potential rise and the phenomenal growth in software sector need to assure and ensure the knowledge workers with the economic benefit, which is the undercurrent in the new paradigm of "online knowledge market". In the make fit arrangement with the traditional copyright law, there is an apparent gap in protecting the intangible transitional plasticity and transmissibility of the digital creations. The Convergence Bill 2001 need be better debated holistically to make it apt and synchronize the issues to meet the impeding challenges the country is likely to face with the growing use and application of the Internet, the generously generated software packages and applications. Care need be taken that there are no violations of IPR regime from with the country and at the same time to provide the safeguard and security for the generated Intellectual Property.

11

Copyright In The Digital Environment: A State of the Art Report

K. N. Prasad

Introduction

Intellectual Property Right connotes the rights to literary, artistic and scientific work; performances of performing artists; phonograms and broadcasts; inventions in all fields of human endeavor; scientific discoveries, industrial designs; trademarks, service mark and commercial names and designations; and all other products resulting from intellectual activity in the industrial, scientific, literary and artistic fields. It is a generic term covering patent, registered design, trademark, copyright, layout of integrated circuits, trade secrets, geographical indicators and anti-competitive practices in contractual licenses.

Librarians and copyright

Librarians and information professionals recognize, and are committed to support the needs of their patrons to gain access to copyright works and the information and ideas they contain. They also respect the needs of authors and copyright owners to obtain a fair economic return to their intellectual property. Effective access is essential in achieving copyright's objectives.

Copyright law impacts on most of what libraries do. It affects the services that libraries can provide to their users, and the conditions on which they can provide access to copyright materials. It affects the way in which libraries can act as navigational agents and undertake effective archiving and preservation activities.

Libraries have crucial role to play in controlling as well as facilitating access to the increasing number of local and remote electronic information resources. Librarians and information professionals promote respect for copyright and actively defend copyright works against piracy, unfair use and unauthorized exploitation, in the digital environment. Libraries have long acknowledged that they have a role in informing and educating users about the importance of copyright law and in encouraging compliance.

Today, it is widely believed that personal computers, cable television, the Internet and the telephone system are converging into a giant hose that will spray huge amounts of data – intellectual property. As this occurs, according to the conventional scenario, the economic winners will be those who own the zeroes and ones, not those who make equipment that copies, transmits and displays them. Because copyright is the mechanism for establishing ownership, it is increasingly seen as the key to wealth in the information Age.

At the same time the transformation of intellectual property into electronic form creates new problems. If the cost of manufacturing and distributing a product falls, economic forces will drive down its price too. The net embodies this principle to an extreme degree.

In addition creators deal with piracy, which is vastly easier and more effective in the digital environment. People have long been able to photocopy texts, tape record music and videotape television shows. If the document (film) is digitized into a computer file, it can be e-mailed to millions of people in minutes; because strings of zeroes and ones can be reproduced with absolute fidelity, the copies are perfect. And online pirates have no development costs. In other words, even as a digital technology drives the potential value of copyright to even greater heights, the same technology threatens to make it next to worthless.

The paradox has created two situations. One is to advocate eliminating copyright altogether. Anticopyrightists believe that the increased ease of copying effectively obviates the © symbol and all it entails. In this view, copyright restricts what people can do with the intellectual property coming through the wires. It tries to fence the electronic frontier. It unjustly creates monopolies in the basic commodity of the Information Age. The other opposing reaction is to strengthen the hands of copyright owners.

The Library Association Copyright Alliance (LACA) of UK supports the effective enforcement of copyright and recognizes that libraries, information services and archives have a crucial role to play in controlling as well as facilitating access to the increasing number of local and remote electronic information resources.

LACA maintains that over protection of copyright could threaten democratic traditions and impact on social justice principles by unreasonably restricting access to information and knowledge. If copyright protection is too strong, competition and innovation is restricted and creativity is stifled.

If in future all access and use of information in digital format becomes subject to payment, a library's ability to provide access to its users will be severely restricted in order to maintain a balance between the interests of rights holders and users.

LACA Statement of principles

1. For works in digital format, without incurring a charge or seeking permission all users of a library should be able to:
   - browse publicly available copyright material;
   - read, listen to, or view publicly marketed copyright material privately, on site or remotely;
   - copy or have copied for them by library and information staff, a reasonable portion of digital work in copyright for personal, or educational use.
2. Providing access to digital format of a protected work to user for a legitimate purpose, such as research or study should be permitted under copyright law.
3. The lending of published physical format digital materials (for example CD-ROMs) by libraries should not be restricted by legislation.

4. Contractual provisions, for example, within licensing agreements, should not override reasonable lending of electronic resources by library staff.
5. Legislation should give libraries and archives permission to convert copyright protected materials into digital format for preservation and conservation related purposes.
6. Legislation should also cover the legal deposit of electronic media.
7. National copyright legislation should render invalid any terms of a license that restrict or override exceptions or limitations embodied in copyright law where the license is established unilaterally by the rightsholders without the opportunity for negotiation of the terms of the license by the user.
8. National copyright laws should aim for a balance between the rights of copyright owners to protect their interests through technical means and the rights of users to circumvent such measures for legitimate, non-infringing purposes.
9. Copyright law should enunciate clear limitations on liability of third parties in circumstances where compliance cannot practically or reasonably be enforced.

In the world of Internet, a common practice is to forward e-mail messages, or portion thereof; to quote portions of Usenet and mailing list postings; and to make private non-commercial copies of texts downloaded from ftp, gopher, or web sites. Under current definitions of fair use, these practices would be considered fair uses; and they are also acceptable norms of practice for Internet users. Grey areas of fair use and potential copyright infringement activities would include:

- Scanning of photographs in GIF formats (these are usually copyrightable images; for instance a common Usenet practice is to scan in Playboy photographs, but these images are protected by copyright);
- Typing in newspaper or magazine articles (acceptable to type in portions with the correct citation and attribution);

- Posting articles or private e-mail written by someone else without their express permission.

Network culture must create a culture where fair use is understood alongside a level of compliance and responsibility, or else fair use will be stifled and negotiating fees and licenses will become the norm.

In the United States, the National Information Infrastructure (NII) Preliminary Report, the Green Paper on "Intellectual Property and the National Information Infrastructure" was released by the Working Group on Intellectual Property Rights in July 1994. The Paper recommended that the Copyright Act of 1976 be amended slightly to accommodate the advent of digital information. The paper recommended that:

- Digital transmission of a copy of a copyrighted work be considered an act of copyright infringement;
- 'First sale' rules for works transmitted digitally be abolished;
- Copyright infringement could be constructed if technological devices are used to circumvent copy-protection schemes that copyright owners have created.

Four areas of copyright law and their applicable to digital transmission have been identified by the Green Paper. They include: right to browse; right of digital transmission; abolishment of first sale rule; and abolishment of fair use.

Copyright issues in the digital environment are global, not local issues. How can differing national laws and dictums be harmonized in the global context? Many commentators have suggested that a copyright clearing house to issue licenses and cleat rights will become a necessary adjunct to creating multimedia content on the information highway.

"The primary objective of copyright is not to reward the labor of authors, but 'to promote the progress of science and useful arts'.

Copyright : Internet

Copyright has been the focus of protecting intellectual property on the Internet. As such, there have been both technological and legislative efforts to continue incentives for authors to create useful works.

Contributory infringement (and the consequent liability) is one of the most contentious areas of the copyright debate. For instance, is an ISP liable for contributory infringement when it allows its users to link to hacker sites? If an ISP closed a user's account when informed by an IP owner, would the ISP be liable for the violation of civil rights or breach of contract?

Bandwidth on the network is limited, and continues to be so. The traditional technical solution, caching, is to allow copies to be saved at distributed points throughout the network. However, caching raises two issues. First cached copies can be out of date yet still contains information which is time sensitive (such as prices or stock quotes). Second, some web sites derive revenue based on the amount and kind of access to their servers, and they currently have no verifiable way of counting the number of access to their servers, their document cached elsewhere on the network.

Copyright: databases

Databases as a concept has undergone a change after Internet has narrowed the distances for transacting business. Databases were initially seen primarily as stored information say, in the form of share prices, details of employees, products and such other information. Today the term databases constitute data stored in the World Wide Web, CDs, multimedia products, network and so on.

Both the quality and quantity of the data has gained a lot of significance with the development of knowledge sharing which evolved with computer era.

The voluminous information being created everyday has highlighted the need for protection of databases. On account of this, adequate protection of databases has become very important.

The object of such a protection is to ensure:

- That the owner gets his right to protect the data adequately;

- Accessibility of the data to all those who legitimately wish to use the same;
- Prohibition of unauthorized use of data.

One of the best ways of protection of databases is by adhering to Intellectual Property Rights (IPR). In databases, copyright vests as soon as a database or any data for that matter, is created.

In India, copyright is available, for the form and the substance of the matter. However, any infringer can intelligently change the arrangement of preexisting database and reuse the same material thereby avoiding the copyright law.

The fact that "bits" of a new database can consist of pieces from other copyrighted material is causing a lot of concern among the academic community and there have been calls for pressure to be put on governments to loosen such restrictions.

Software patentability is controversial and goes two-ways for the seller and the buyer (user). It should be noted that there is a need to pay the fees of any software used, to pay royalties to the right holders of client software.

Copyright-Digital format

One can produce perfect copies from works in digital format. When anybody downloads a digital work and prints or makes disk copies, each of these copies is a perfect copy. While accessibility can be increased because of the availability of digital formats, it also makes private copying of these works easier and more difficult to detect.

Copyright owners certainly want to preserve and expand their markets. However, not all authors share these same values; for example, academic authors often want wide dissemination of their works and are not so much concerned about market protection.

Because copyright works become part of the social record of a civilization public access is especially important to librarians. The licensing digital resources as opposed to purchase of the work threatens public access, a core value for the public at large.

Information needs to be communicated and shared to be valuable. Certainly, copyright holders deserve fair compensation for their works, but licensing may or may not be fair.

One of the significant differences between analog and digital works is that one can use a non-electronic work without making a copy of that work. If the work is in digital format, this is not true.

It is suggested that copyright law's focus on making a copy may simply no longer be relevant since access by computer by their nature make copies, but these ephemeral copies are not significant and should not be considered infringing copies. It is also suggested that copyright protection could be reexamined to consider how copyright could function without the notion of copying.

Copyrighted works are protected regardless of the medium in which they are created or reproduced; thus, copyright extends to digital works and works transformed into a digital format. Copyrighted works are not limited to those that bear a copyright notice. As a result of changes in copyright law, works published since March 1, 1989 need not bear a copyright notice to be protected under the statute.

The digital and networked environment has posed several problems to the copyright law. This is because:

a. **In the digital medium, works are more equivalent:** In digital form, all copyrighted works-pictures, sounds, texts, music or movies – consist of strings of bits. All therefore, fit the definition of "literary work."

b. **The plasticity of works in digital form:** Works in digital form are easily transformed form one form to another. They are also easy to alter, even without a change in the character of the work. With the right tools, it is easy to digitally edit photographs, texts, or anything else – and to do so in a manner which cannot easily be detected.

c. **Automatic generation of works in digital form:** The digital medium also permits new works to be created for which no human author can readily be designated.

d. **Technological and contractual means for overcoming digital replicability:** An well – recognised problem digital technologies pose for copyright arises from the ease and low cost with which multiple copies can be made and distributed in digital form, especially in a networked environment.

Copyright in the digital environment

New communications technologies bring unprecedented opportunities for improving access to information and technology has the potential to improve communication and access for those disadvantaged by distance or economic circumstances. However, we now know that technology also has the potential to further stratify society into the information-haves and the information-have-nots. If reasonable access to copyright works is not maintained in the digital environment, a further barrier will be erected which will deny access to those who cannot afford to pay.

WIPO

In 1996, the members of the World Intellectual Property Organisation adopted two treaties to update copyright law for the digital environment. In confirming that existing exceptions and limitations can be carried forward and extended in the digital environment, WIPO countries rejected the claim that "digital is different". Contracting parties are allowed to carry forward and extend such limitations in the digital environment, and create new exceptions where appropriate.

IFLA

IFLA is an international non-governmental organisation (NGO) which exists to undertake, support and co-ordinate research and studies, and disseminate information about all aspects of library and information work world wide and to organise meetings and training in this field.

Traditionally, libraries have been able to provide reasonable access to the purchased copies of copyright works held in their collections. However, if in future all access and use of information in digital format becomes subject to payment, a library's ability to provide access to its users will be severely restricted In order to maintain a balance between the interests of rights holders and users, IFLA has developed the following statement of principles.

Statement of Principles

1. In national copyright legislation, exceptions to copyright and related rights, allowed in the Berne Convention and endorsed by the WIPO treaties should be revised if necessary to ensure that permitted uses apply equally to information in electronic form and information in print.
2. For copying over and above these provisions there should be administratively simple payment schemes.
3. Temporary or technical copies which are incidental to the use of copyright material should be excluded from the scope of the reproduction right.
4. For works in digital format, without incurring a charge or seeking permission all users of a library should be able to:
   - browse publicly available copyright material;
   - read, listen to, or view publicly marketed copyright material privately, on site or remotely;
   - copy, or have copied for them by library and information staff, a reasonable portion of a digital work in copyright for personal, educational or research use.
5. Providing access to a digital format of a protected work to a user for a legitimate purpose such as research or study should be permitted under copyright law.
6. The lending of published physical format digital materials (for example CD ROMs) by libraries should not be restricted by legislation.
7. Contractual provisions, for example, within licensing arrangements, should not override reasonable lending of electronic resources by library staff.
8. Legislation should give libraries and archives permission to

convert copyright protected materials into digital format for preservation and conservation related purposes.

9. Legislation should also cover the legal deposit of electronic media.
10. National copyright legislation should render invalid any terms of a license that restrict or override exceptions or limitations embodied in copyright law where the license is established unilaterally by the right holders without the opportunity for negotiation of the terms of the license by the user.
11. National copyright laws should aim for a balance between the rights of copyright owners to protect their interests through technical means and the rights of users to circumvent such measures for legitimate, non-infringing purposes.
12. Copyright law should enunciate clear limitations on liability of third parties in circumstances where compliance cannot practically or reasonably be enforced.

Electronic copyright management systems (ECMS)

There is no appropriate copyright management system designed to the environment of the web. It has, however, been felt that there is a need for consensus for standards for such a system. We are all used to the notion that copyrighted works are of an intangible nature, and we are trained to make the distinction between the work as such, and a copy that work, the former being an intangible concept, while the latter is physical object. Characteristic for the digital environment is the disappearance of physical copies. A machine readable from is a copy, and one may trade with such copies as is seen in CD-ROMs, where the conventional systems for rights management may be successfully applied. But for business in the digital environment, copies are not traded. The trade in physical objects is replaced by a trade in signs liberated from the media on which the signs more or less incidentally are stored, more or less temporarily. But here, there is a copy of the work. He may use it for personal benefit but also for re-distribution through an intranet.

Several attempts have been made at developing Electronic Copyright Management Systems (ECMS).One important effort is CITED (Copyright in Transmitted Electronic Documents) a project producing a generic model of how to achieve a solution for digital environment under which two demonstrators were implanted – ADONIS for a collection of journals in machine readable form, and NRCISSE for fine art from several museums with accompanying explanatory texts. IMPRIMATUR is another current project attracting lot of attention.

DEVELOPMENT OF ECMS

The elements necessary for the development of a viable electronic copyright management system may be:

- Identification: Identifiers are well known in the conventional environment Eg. International Standard Book Number (ISBN). A better example is the International Standard Recording Code (ISRC) which was developed by the International Standards Organization (ISO), as an identifier for phonograms and audiovisual recordings known as ISO 3901. There are currently efforts in developing such codes for many categories of works. They are often referred to as " Copyright management information". The code will typically be a reference to a database that contains the details of the work, for instance the owner, or succession of owners, the licensing divided on geographical areas, media, etc.
- A related method is that of fingerprinting which is a scheme for retaining information on the use of the work. There is emerging scheme of identifying each work by a code embedded in the work itself, a code which may be retrieved by a copyright management system, and used as a key for accessing databases containing detailed information on the rights associated with this work, for instance for distributing revenues.
- **Cryptography:** To protect the work, it should be subjected to encryption. This would make it possible only for somebody

with access to the key to benefit from the works. The technology allows many legal issues to be solved, obviously identification and authentication of the parties are secured.

- **Payment:** It is important to find a scheme that allows on the spot purchases of items of rather low value.
- **User identification:** There must be some way of ensuring the identity of the user.

The transaction is indicated by the user who identifies a work he or she wants to purchase. The material is not necessarily residing on a database under the control of the right holder, as it is in encrypted form and therefore protected in this way. The system would rather identify and authenticate the end user, checking that the necessary credit is available at the account of the end user. It would retrieve the copyright management information from the work, perhaps accessing a database to determine how the payment should be distributed. The work would then be transferred to the user and decrypted by his device, at the same time the payment would be deducted from his or her account and credited to appropriate account of the right holders.

Copyright, digital environment, India

The Information Technology Bill-1999 which has been introduced in the parliament during November 1999 is a giant step to take India ahead in the new Internet era.

The protection of content on Internet, which in all its form covers the classic definition of IPR and Copyright Act, however, does not find a proper mention in the new IT Act given assent by the President.

The content on the Internet is the parameter for the success of any dot com. It is the back bone of the Internet business and IPR is related to it. Ironically care has not been taken about IPR issue in the IT Bill, which could prove fatal in the long term. Experts observe that the responsibility on the contents should be with the producer and not with ISP providers who act just as middlemen.

Some, however, feel that being a web host ISP has responsibility to provide content after proper scrutiny.

It is unusual for authors of articles in scholarly journals to receive any recompense for their work. Many, if not most, authors assign rights to their work to the publisher without taking into account of such material might subsequently appear in other media.

Given the development of electronic journals however, perhaps it is time to look again at such issues as fair use, the relationship between information and intellectual property, copyright and the economic ramifications of the new technology, some moves in the direction have already been made.

Computer crimes recognized under this law would affect hackers and those who are not authorized to enter a system to download data, introduce viruses, damage data or the system, block access to authorized users.

The law would apply to anyone in or outside of India who tampers with a computer located in India.

Conclusion

The answers to the questions like : Does the nature of the technology require us to change the legal understanding or status of copyright as it stands now? What rights should be associated with to Web content?; and How should the rights be expressed, and should the expression of the rights be used for notification, enforcement, or payment negotiation? – does not necessarily lie solely in technology nor policy, but the rational combination of both.

IPR is something that affects us every day. We should be conscious of its effects on our economy. It is not enough to have strong laws but strong mechanisms to enforce, like the judiciary, police and the customs.

It remains to be seen whether strict adherence to copyright laws is possible. If it is going to be meaningful protection, it has to be done on a global basis through international treaties that all nations are prepared to recognize and follow.

References

1. Anuradha. K. T. Copyright fair use and database in digital networked environment. In *National Seminar on Information Policies and Cyber laws*, 4-6 December 2000. Bangalore, Sarada Ranganathan Endowment for Library Science. Paper E.
2. Ivey, Keith C. *New Copyright legislation* (http://www.eeicommunications.com)
3. Prasad, K. N. Intellectual Property Rights. *Information Studies* Vol. 4 (2); 1998; p. 67-104
4. Intellectual Property Rights in India : An overview. In *National Seminar on Information Policies and Cyber laws*, 4-6 December 2000, Bangalore, Sarada Ranganathan Endowment for Library Science, PAPER A.

12

Copyright As A Intellectual Property And Information Technology

J. V. Joshi

Objectives

The objective of present paper is to review the development of the concept of copyright and its significance in the globalization perspective. The paper is also intended to focus the significance of applicability of the concept in an information technology oriented environment.

Meaning of Copyright

It would not be out of place at the outset to clarify what is meant by the term copyright. Literally the term "copyright" comprises of two factors viz. "copy" and "right" that is to say it is the right to copy something what this something is left to be interpreted by the statute. The Encyclopaedic Dictionary of Library and Information Science defines a copyright as........ " the right to prevent publication, statute have extended the defination to include the right to prevent multiplication as the form of copies by what so ever means.

Encylopaedia Britanica writes " A copyright is the exclusive legally secured right to publish reproduce & sell the matter & form of a literary, musical, dramatic, or artistic work." "Copyright is designed primarly to protect an artist, publisher or other owner against any unathorised copying or his work......" For the purpose of understanding the concept of copyright in the prespective of an information technology era one must first understand the concept of intellectual property.

Tibor Gold (1991) has rightly remarked "It is in principle, like all other property. It is owned by its originater, who may by contract of employment or by contract of transfer pass ownership to some onelse." The term intellectual property is a wide term comprehensive enough to cover different kinds of intellectual properties such as design, pattern, trademark, etc. & also includes the concept of copyright. Roger Broadle (1991) explaining the term says "copyright is the most pervasive of all the intellectual property rights. It protects a wide range of the material, a company proudues reports, manuals, production drawings, computer programs, publicity materials, and even its correspondence. The copyright of materials like these is one of a company's most important intellectual property assets."

Origin of the concepts

The History of the concept of copyright can be traced back to 15th century when this concept was for the first time reconginsed in the City of Venice. During the 16th century, England adopted this concept. The first statute regarding copyright is the Statued of Anne passed in England in 1710 AD. This regulation proved to be an important land mark in the history of the concept of copyright .This law asserted for the first time the Author primary right for copy & publication of a literary work. Thereafter similar laws were framed in Denmark (1741), United States (1790), & France (1793), it should be noted that no separate statute was framed in India. In 1955 Universal Copyright Convention came in to existence. The main object of this convention was to gain worldwide support for the concept of copyright, It attempted to gain support from the members of Berne Convention & other inter American Convention. In 1952 59 countries, under the quspices of UNESCO had sighed a multilateral agreement which recognised the concept of copyright. Copyright protects all types of work, The latest development being that, in 1988 in UK. Copyright Designe & Patents Act 1988 was passed. This act now works as guiding principle for understanding the concept of copyright. It should be noted that copyright arises automatically. It is created as soon as a particular work i.e. book, design, document etc. is created No formalitles like registration etc. are involved &

no professional guidance or expertise is needed. Normally following items are covered under the concept of copyright.

- Literary, dramatic, musical & artistic works.
- Sound recordings, films broadcasts, cable programming & the typrographical arrigements of published editions.

Changing Economic Environment

The business environment is an ever changing fact. The liberlisation of Indian economy has laid to a shift in the mind set of Indian business community. The process of liberliation has open the doors of the economy for multinational. The watershade year was 1991, when India started the process of reforming its economy & integrating it with the global economy. This has ultered the sitation has been rishtly remark "The world is beconing a global market characterised by economic inter-dependence & emergence of large economic blocks like EEC, ASEAN,SAFTA, NAFTA and Central American Common Market etc.The important devekopment of glopal market is the resurgence of market forces imparting tremendous impact on all spheres Techonlogies Economics social political & cultural. The national boundares have becomes less signfficant with the inter-linked effect of technology information flows & foreign investiment mobiligy" Thus the changing state of economy under the process of globalisation has created the necessity of proper understanding of the concept of copyright. It has been rightly remarked by Viven Irish the concept of intellectual property has recently qcquired much prominence. Industrial managers have long appreciated the value of ideas, their exploltation has largely been a fringe consideration patenting has more often been intended as protection of a domestic market rather than as a sprongboard for growth. The internationalization of trade & the growing need for collaboration in research with other companies, including potential competitors, has forced all those seriously involved in the business of innovation to examine their procedures. Thus it can be seen that the concept of intellectual property which includes the concept of copyright has become a major source of the progress of nation & the concept has been global perspective.

Copyright & GATT

The Uruguey round of multilateral trade negotiation (MTN) was the eight in a series of multilateral trade negotiations conducted under the auspices of the General Agreement and Tarifs & Trase (GATT) The negotiations were to cover a wide range of issues & were for more ambitious than any MTN's carried out eariler. The traditional concern of such negotàtions has generally been a liberalization of trade . The Uruguey Round went beyond that. It talked of the rules & disciplines of the trading system. It also visualised discussions in new areas like trade in services, Trade.-Related Intellectual Property Rights (TRIPS) & Trade Related Investment Measures (TRIMS) P.R. Sivasankar has rightly remarked "TRIPS form the part of trade in services which is included for the first time in GATT negotiation. This highly contentius issue attracted overwhelming cristisim from both opposition parties & academicians in India." As copy right is covered under the perview of TRIPS It is expected that GATT agreement would have a notable impact upon a concept of copyright .

Copyright & Information Technology

With the advent of information technology & wide spread use of computers the electronic data processing instument have became major source of knowledge creation in the form of words, sounds & designer. Naturally a question arises as to whether a computer generator work is subject to copyright or not & if it is, what type of works created by IT instrument are covered under protection & what type of protection is available. Although it was generally accepted for many years in the United Kingdom that computer programs were protected by copyright that fact was not confirmed by legislation until the Copyright (Computer Software), Amendment Act 1985 one of its purposes was to increase the penalties for commercial piracy of computer programs, but at the same time it confirmed the status of all computers programs, including those existing at that time as works protected under copyright they were to be treated in the same way as literary works was left undecided.

The 1988 Act has put the exact nature of computer programs as copyright works beyond doubt. They are now stated to be literary works. Consequently all the general provisions concering literary works will also apply to a computer programe. Thus, to enjoy copyright the program must be orignal ownership will normally vest in the programmer or if the programmer is employed in the employer. The 1988 Act does not define "computer program for fear that any defination might exclude forms of computer program that will developed in the future. The statute of the United State defines a computer program as " a set of statements or instructions to be used directly or indirectly in a computer in order to bring about a certain result." There is an overwhelming international consensus, confirmed by court decisions of leglslation in many countries that computer programs should be protected by copyrights. There are two main reasons. First copyright gives a suitable level of protection for a work that takes much skill & effort to develop but which can be copied at negligible expense second it ensure a uniform international recognition through the regularements of the Berne Convention & avoids the uncertainity which would result from any attempt to develop a special-purpose from of protection. The European Commision has accepted the idea of protecting a computer program in has prepeared a proposer for legal protection of computer program however the same is yet to be accepted by the council of ministers of UK.

Type of Program that can be covered under copyright.

A number of works, programes & software have been covered under the scope of the term copyright some such program are

- Computer generated works
- Computer generated desing documents
- Database
- Remote acess data based
- Cable program
- Documentation

Now a days many works are created with the help of computer examples are designs produced using a computer, aided designs package & even documents produced on a word processor. In these cases, the computer is acting merely as a tool & the charaetersires of the final work derived from the creative decisions & efforts of the user of the computer. Copyright will attach to the work in the normal way, & the author will be the person who uses the computer. Normally a computer generator work has been define as a work generated by computer in circumstances such that there is no human author of the work. Generally following infringements are availables.

- Electonic Storage
- Distrubuting a computer program
- Loading a computer program
- Running a computer program
- Adaptations
- Rental right
- Transmission
- Criminal offences
- Copy protection.

Conclusion

Thus it can be concluded that computer programes are protected by copyright. The formation of cyber laws & the proposed information technology will should be made comprehensive enough to cover computer program. The signifienace has been eightly recognised in a comprehensive study conducted by George Kodpmaan & Hans Eckart Scharnar of Humburg Istitute for Economic Research on International Trade after Uruguay Round of GATT reveals that "The International protection of intellectual property right (Patent,s Trademark Models, designs, copyrights etc.) is exetnded beyond existing international convention under the umbrella of World Intellectual Property Organization (WIPO) & supplemented with protective measures against product duplicating. Howerer the main regulations of the agrements on Trade Related aspects of Intellectual property Right (TRIPS) is that members effectively enforce the protective standard on a national level including penal majors in the case of product counter felting & copyrights piarcy.

References

1. The Encyclopeadic Dictionary of Library & Information Science Vol 1, Anmol, New Delhi 1995.
2. Encyclopedia of Britanica Vol 3.
3. International Trade after the Urugway Round of the GATT Vol . 52, Institute of Scientific. Cooperation Tubengin Germany.
4. Batra & Dangwal : Interntion Busienss : New Trends Deep & Deep, New Delhi, 1999.
5. Batra & Kaur : GATT Implications of Dunkel Proposals : Anmol, New Delhi, 1994.
6. Shiva Swamy : Gobalisation the Indian Scenario : Bangalore, 1996.
7. Viven Irish : Intellectual Property A managers Guide : McGraw Hill, 1991, UK.

Section 3
Violation of Copyrights and Librarianship

13

COPYRIGHT: INTERPRETING THE LAW FOR LIBRARIES

N. J. Deshpande

Only technologically advanced nations are dominating economically these days. We can find a number of cases of interdependence of nations in trade & technology. With limited resources available at the disposal of a nation is suggestive and logical during current times to seek economic growth through technology transfer. In the areas of dissemination of information number of documents are in the form of electronic. The most prominent consideration these days is the protection of intangible assets, more specifically the intellectual property rights.

The idea behind copyright is rooted in certain fundamental ideas about creativity and possession. Anything we create is an extension of 'self' and should be protected from general use by anyone else. The person creating something has exclusive rights over the thing created for at least two reasons. First, it could be argued, an absence of such a protection would discourage human creativity and thereby development of the world both culturally and technically. Second, there seems to be some moral or ethical grounds for believing the person should be entitled to enjoy the economic or other fruits of his or her labors. The absence of intellectual property rights damages creativity or industry.

It is quite difficult job to define intellectual property. A useful stating point is that intellectual property comprises all those things that come from the human intellect, whether they are ideas, inventions, words (fact and fiction), music, theater or art. More specifically in the context of the information, this would include material such as databases (whether online, CD-ROM or delivered by other mechanisms), individual item in a database, computer software, and all manner of printed and microfilm materials.

Role of Government

Government projects intellectual property in terms of penalties for infringement, through to different manner of tests and hurdles that one must overcome if one is to protect one's intellectual property.

The Trade Related Intellectual Property Rights (TRIPs) is a comprehensive treaty formed after detailed discussions on IPR held at an international forum constituted for multilateral trade negotiations. The said treaty provides the norms and standards for protection of intellectual property during trading transactions. The TRIPs is the outcome of eight rounds of discussions held under General Agreement on Trade and Tariffs (GATT) by its member nations. Now TRIPs stand adopted by the majority of nations in the world. Its total membership has gone up to 136 nations. It is one of the major developments of the present century having far reaching implications for world economy. To understand its implications for the member nations, it is better to first go into the background of its evolution.

To reshape the world economy after great depression (1929-32) and the Second World War (1939-45), the GATT was set up on 30th October, 1947 at Geneva (Switzerland) with an initial membership of 23 countries. It became operative with effect from 1st January 1948. The GATT was a sort of ad hoc body created for the purpose of carrying out multilateral trade negotiations among members. Up to the year 1993, eight rounds of negotiations were completed under the GATT arrangement. During the intervening period of GATT's life it has made some remarkable achievements in the form of increase in membership, expert growth, imports tariff reductions and increase in the volume international trade. The first seven rounds of talks held under GATT were of short duration with specific agenda focused on tariff reductions and other minor issues.

However, the eighth round that was conducted at Uruguay from Sept. 1986 to Dec. 1993 was the most comprehensive one and touched almost all issues concerning international trade. On Dec. 20, 1991 the then Director General of GATT, Arthur Dunkel, Prepared a comprehensive document of 433 pages making series of proposals in as Many as 28 areas concerning international trade. This document is popularly known as 'Dunkel Draft' and become the basis for all further negotiations. The Dunkel Draft initially roused lot of controversies particularly in developing countries including India, but finally it was accepted and 117 countries put their signatures to Uruguay Final Act in Murrakesh, Morocco, on 15th of April 1994. India was one of the signatories to this treaty.

As an outcome of the eighth round of GATT, the World Trade Organization (WTO), a permanent legal institution as a replacement to GATT, come into being and become operative with effect from 1st January 1995. The WTO assumed the role of a watchdog of world trade with the objectives of encouraging the growth of the most competitive location to produce goods and services, thereby, ensuring the most efficient use of global resources. The other key areas on which agreements were finalized at the conclusion of the eighth round include Agricultural Sector, Tariff levels, General Agreement on Trade in Services (GATS), Agreement on Subsidies and countervailing measures. Thus TRIPs evolved as one of the measures to regulate world trade. India has signed this agreement. Now, implementation of the provisions of TRIPs is one of the key concerns of the WTO. India in the present situations is left with no option but to take necessary measures to comply with the requirements of the provisions of TRIPs to keep pace with the rest of the world and take maximum possible advantages out of it.

Literary Works

What sorts of works are covered by copyright by the term literary works? Anything that is written, printed or recorded in some other way can be the subject of such copyright protection. The owner's copyright rights, preventing others from doing certain acts, are limited in various in various ways. Copyrights are granted for literary, dramatic, musical, artistic, cinematographic film and sound recording works. Computer programming and software works are covered in the category of literary works only.

What is not protected by copyright?

- Works that have not been fixed in a tangible from of expression (for ex choreographic works that have not been noted or recorded or speeches or performances that have not been written or recorded.)
- Titles, names, short phrases and slogans; familiar symbols or designs, more variations of typographic ornamentation, lettering or coloring, mere listing of ingredients or contents.
- Ideas, procedures, methods, systems, processes, concepts, principles, discoveries or devices, as distinguished from a description, explanation or illustration.
- Works consisting entirely of information that is common property and containing no original authorship (for example, standard calendars, height & weight charts, tape measures and rulers and lists or tables taken from public documents or other common sources.

Copyright is secured automatically when the work is created, and a work is "created" when it is fixed in a copy or phonorecord for the first time.

In USA under the 1976 Copyright Act defines the Publication as follows – "Publication" is the distribution of copies or phonorecords of a work to the public by sale or other transfer of ownership, or by rental, lease, or lending. The offering to distribute copies or phonorecords to a group of persons for purposes of further distribution, public performance, or public display constitutes publication. A public performance or display of a work does not of itself constitute publication.

It is clear that any form of dissemination in which the material object does not change hands, for ex. Performances or displays on television, is not a publication or matter how many people are exposed to the work. However, when copies or phonorecords are offers for sale or lease to a group of wholesalers, broadcasters, or motion picture theaters, publication does take place if the purpose is further distribution, public performance or public display.

There is a special type of literary work called compilations. This is a collection of works, each of which may or may be subject to individual copyright. The collection or compilation has in many countries its own copyright because skill and efforts were expended in making the collection. In addition, many countries have special arrangements too for government copyright and parliamentary copyright.

Copyright in India are granted under the Copyright Act, 1957, as amended in 1983, 1984, 1992 and 1994 and the Copyright Rules, 1958. It is interesting to point out that India's copyright laws are quite exhaustive and are in tune with the requirements of TRIPs. India has also set up a Copyright Enforcement Advisory Council to strengthen the enforcement of the rules. The period for which copyright remains valid varies from work to work. For literary works the copyright validity period is the whole life of the author plus sixty-year if work is published during the lifetime of the author. For sound recording the copyright is for a period of twenty-five years and for the remaining category of works, the period is against sixty years.

So here, we have a literary work, whether in print or machine-readable form. Copyright law says no one may copy it – and copying includes photocopying, converting it into machine readable form, downloading data from it, faxing it, and microfilming it. Librarian and information scientists are able to do these things to a limited extent because of important exceptions to the rule about not being able to copy. I want to look at the most important of this exception: fair use. Fair use means that an individual may make a copy of not too substantial a part of a literary work as long as the copying does not damage the legitimate interests of the copyright owner and as long as it is for one of the purposes specified in the local legislation. Typically, national legislations will permit fair use (known in some countries as "fair dealing") for one or more of the following reasons:

research, private study, criticism and book reviewing, reporting current events, and educational purposes. Most library and information uses fall under the heading of "research or private study". Fair use begs many questions. For example, what is "substantial"? Local new offers no guidelines, and there are very few court decisions to rely on. It all depends on the particular circumstances. What about "research and private study? The term is fairly self-explanatory, though it is worth stressing that research and private study is not just linked to formal courses of study, but for any private purpose. In most countries, "research" can be academic research, industrial research, or any other sort, whether for profit or not.

Librarians and Information Scientist often download from online & CD-ROM databases. What is the impact of copyright on database producers, online hosts and those people who use online hosts and CD-ROMS to retrieve information? This not simple as it might seem. The content a database is protested as a literary work but the database service is protected differently. If a work is purely an in-house database created on PC on an individual's desk or one such as that created in a large company or local authority, than it is a literary work. If the database in one available to the public purely for viewing or for searching, then it becomes a cable programme and is not literary work.

It law does not recognize the term database, the content of any work is treated according to its nature. The term compilation would fit most of the database.

The author of the content of an electronic work will be decided in the same way as if that work were not electronic. Databases rarely have personal authors. They are, therefore, regarded as anonymous unless they are fulltext databases where items are separately identified. For computer program, the person who wrote the program is the author.

Essentially databases will be protected in the same way as literary work but, because of the uncertainty of their status in copyright law in some European countries a special right called Sui generis will be introduced. This gives protection to a database.

To conclude it may be said that development of new forms of publication, which is the essential subject of copyright, has already made obsolete many ideas as to the law of copyright inherited form the past CD ROM, computer programming, sound recording are not amenable to rules of law developed in the eighteenth countries for the protection of documents. These and other scientific developments will determine the shape of copyright law for the future, for the law must necessarily respond to needs national consensus be created on such sensitive issues which have far reaching implications for the economy of the country. In creased public awareness can perhaps better help the process of consensus formulation.

References

1. Narayana, P.S.: Intellectual Property Law in India Hyerabad, Gogia Law Agency, 2000, 855p.
2. Cornish, Grahm, P.: Copyright, London Library Association1998, 189p.
3. Keilhoffer A.R. & Wisely, C.L. : HELDA help desk Assistance, 1990, 57-59p

14

Violation Of Copyrights: Why And How

Prakash G. Karmarkar

Introduction

Violation of Copyrights means in other language infringement of Copyright Act. Copyright is not the mere creature of structure but a natural and civil right, though under the present Act It is a creature of statute. It is property right.

After the passing of the Copyright Act 1957, Copyright exists solely by virtue of the Act. Copyright at common law gets merged into statutory copyright and there is no copyright now in any work, published or unpublished apart from that conferred by the statute. First of all, we must try to understand what is infringement. Copyright in any work is deemed to be infringed.

a. When any person without a license from the owner of the copyright, or the register of copyright, or in contravention of the condition of a license granted or any conditions imposed by a competent authority under the act.

    i. Does anything, exclusive right to do which is conferred upon the owner of the copyright or

    ii. Permits for profit any place to be used for the communication of the work to the public where such communication constitutes an infringement of the copyright in the work, unless he was not aware and has no reasonable ground for believing that such communication to the public would be an infringement of copyright, or

b. Where a person,

i. Makes for sale or hire, or spells or lets for hire or by way of trade displays or offers for sale or hire any infringing copies of the work, or

ii. Distributes, either for the purpose of trade or such an extent as to affect prejudicially the owner of the copyright, any infringing copies of the work, or

iii. Exhibits to public by way of trade any infringing copies of work, or

iv. Imports into India any infringing copies of work except one copy of any work, for the private and domestic use of the importer.

Copyright act provides protection to the intellectual property, The true principle is that a person is not at liberty to use or avail of labor and skill of another for the purpose of producing his work. It has been said that "What is worth copying is worth protecting".

Essential ingredients of infringement depending upon the kind of copyright work, infringement involves one or more of the following acts:

1. Reproduction of the work in a material form.
2. Publication of the work,
3. Communication of the work to the public.
4. Performance of the work in public.
5. Making of adaptations and translations of the work and doing any of the above acts in relation to a substantial part of the work.

To establish infringement it must be shown that the alleged infringing work closely resembles the original work and that use has been made directly of the original work.

The question of infringement may be resolved by comparing the two works as a whole, and determining whether there is not merely an identity or similarity or resemblance in some of the leading features or in certain of the details, but whether keeping in view the idea and general effect created by the original, there is such a degree of identity or similarity as would lead one to say that the alleged infringement is a copy or reproduction of the original. Additions, omissions and modifications do not avoid infringement of copyright.

In some cases there will be no direct evidence of copying. Copying can only be deduced by inference from all the surrounding circumstances. In the case of infringement of literacy works the defendants' work containing the same errors as in the plaintiffs work, similarity in language and idiosyncrasies in style may constitute some evidence of copying.

Here one important point has to be considered, that by the copyright act protection is given to creative works that are musical, literacy, artistic works, lectures, plays, art reproductions, models, photographs, computer software etc. the right under this also have a specified duration of protection. The term of a work, (other than a photographic work or a work of applied art) is calculated on a basis other than the life of a natural person.

Such a term will be a term not less than 50 years from the end of the calendar year of the authorized publications within 50 years from the making of the work.(50 years from the calendar year of making).

For example, the term of protection available to performance is at least 50 years computed from the end of the calendar year when the performance took place.

Propositions Relating to Infringement

Court case (Anand v Delux Films AIR 1978 SC. 1613) The Supreme Court after considering a number of English, Indian and American authorities have laid down the following propositions:

1. There can be no Copyright in an idea, subject matter, themes, plots or historical or legendary facts, and violation of the Copyright in such cases is confined to the form, manner and arrangement and expression of the idea by the author of the Copyright work.
2. Where the same idea is being developed in a different manner, it is manifest that the source being common, similarities are

bound to occur. In such a case the courts should determine whether or not the similarities are on fundamental or substantial aspects or the mode of expression adopted in the copyright work. If the defendants' work is nothing but literal limitations of the copyrighted work with some variations here and there it would amount to violation of the copyright. In other words, in order to be actionable the copy must be substantial and material on which at once leads to the conclusion that the defendant is guilty of an act of piracy.

3. One of the surest and safest test to determine whether or not there has been a violation of copyright is to see whether a spectator or the viewer after having read of seen both the works is clearly of the opinion and gets an unmistakable impression that the subsequent work appears to be a copy of the original.
4. Where the theme is the same but is presented and treated differently so that the subsequent work becomes a completely new work, no question of violation of copyright arises.
5. However, apart from the similarities appearing in the two works there are also material and abroad dissimilarities which negative the intention to copy the original and the coincidences appearing in the two works are clearly incidental, no infringement of the copyright comes into existence.
6. As a violation of copyright amounts to an act of piracy it must be proved by clear and cogent evidence after applying the various tests laid down by the case of law.
7. Whether the question is of the violation of the copyright of stage play by a film producer or director the task of the plaintiff becomes more difficult to prove a piracy. It is manifest that unlike a stage play a film has much broader perspective, wider field and bigger background where the defendants can be introducing a variety of incidents give a color and complexion different from the manner in which the copyrighted work has expressed the idea. Even so if the viewer after seeing

the film is by and large a copy of the original play, violation of the copyright may be said to be proved.

There is no express provision under the Copyright Act 1957 to the effect that a person who authorizes another to carry out an infringement is himself an infringed person. However under section 14 to authorize the doing of any of the acts referred to therein is itself one of the rights of the copyright owner. According to a person who authorizes another to commit infringement himself commits an infringement.

Authorization means sanction, approval or countenance. It can also means permit. Any one who sanctions, approves or countenance an infringement may be liable. Even indirect permission or countenancing of infringement would be sufficient to constitute authorizing. The tort of authorizing a breach of copyright is not complete until the breach that has been authorized has been committed. Sale of instruments of copying like cassettes recorder, organizers of public entertainment etc.

Acts not constituting infringements – Statutory exceptions are,

The Copyright Act provides certain exceptions to infringement. The objects of these exceptions is to enable the reproduction of the work for certain public purposes for encouragement of private study and research and promotion of education. Section 52 gives a long list of acts which do not constitute infringement of copyright. They are as follows:

1. Fair dealing with a literary, dramatic, musical or artistic work, not being computer programme for the purpose of private use including research criticism or review, making copies of computer programme for certain purposes, reporting current events in newspapers and magazines or by broadcasting or in a cinematograph film or by means photographs.
2. Reproduction for judicial proceedings and reports thereof, reproduction exclusively for the use of members of legislature,

reproduction (artistic work is excluded) in a certified copy supplied in accordance with law.

3. Reading or citation in public or extracts i.e. literary or dramatic work:
4. Publication in collection for the use of educational institution in certain circumstances.
5. Reproduction by teacher or pupil in the course of instructions or in question papers.
6. Performance in the course of the activities of educational institutions in certain circumstances.
7. The making of sound recording under certain conditions.
8. The causing of a sound recording to be heard in public by utilizing in a closed room or in clubs in certain circumstances.
9. Performance in an amateur club given to a non-paying audience or for religious institutions. .
10. Reproduction in newspaper and magazine of an article on current economic, political, social or religious topics in certain circumstances.
11. Publication in newspaper or magazines a report of a lecture delivered in public.
12. Making a maximum of 3 copies for the use of the public library.
13. Reproduction of unpublished work kept in a museum or library for the purpose of study or research.
14. Reproduction or publication of any matter published in official gazette or reports of govt. commission or other bodies appointed by government.
15. Reproduction of any judgment or order of court, tribunal or other judicial authority not prohibited from publication.
16. Production or publication of a translation of acts of legislature or rules.
17. Making or publishing of painting, drawing or photographs work of a architecture.

18. Making or publishing of painting, drawing or photographs or engraving of sculpture or other artistic work permanently situated in a public place.
19. Inclusion in a cinematograph film of any artistic work permanently situate in a public place and other artistic work by way of background or incidental to the principal matter represented in the film.

Though acts not constituting infringements for above mentioned statutory exceptions; however the publication of the whole work cannot be justified reproduction of a part or whole of the work is permitted for the following purposes.

a. In judicial proceedings or in a report thereof,
b. For the exclusive use of a members of a legislature (state or central).
c. In a certified copy made or supplied in accordance with any law.
d. For teaching or examination purposes. Here academic institutions & their libraries can take advantage of this exception, of course only for teaching and study purpose.
e. For use in newspaper, magazine or periodical of an article of current economic political, social or religious topics unless the author has expressly reserved the right to himself.
f. For use of public libraries (not more than three copies) where the work is not available in India.
g. Reproduction of an unpublished work kept in a library subject to certain conditions.
h. Reproduction or publication of certain government publications.

In the case of infringement of copyright everytime registration of any publishing work is not compulsory, however this is noticed further criminal prosecution of infringement of copyright is sustainable without registration under section 45 of act.

If any person who knowingly infringes or abets infringement of

a. The copyright in a work or

b. Any other right conferred by this Act.

By Act 65 of 1984 section 5 with effect from 8th October 1984 shall be punishable with imprisonment for a term which shall not be less than six months but which may extend to three years and with fine which shall not be less than fifty thousand rupees but which may extend to two lakh rupees except the right conferred by section 53 A. Act 38 of 1994, section 21(2), with effect from 10th May 1995.

References

1. Chaturvedi, R.G. Ed. : Iengar's The Copyright Act, 1957, 6th Ed., New Delhi, Butterworths, 2000.
2. Ganguli, Prabudha : Intellectual Property Rights Unleashing the knowledge Economy, New Delhi, Tata McGraw Hill, 2001.
3. Nair, K.R.G. : Intellectual Property Rights, New Delhi, Allied Pub., 1994.
4. Narayanan, P. : Intellectual property Law 3rd Ed., Kolkata, Eastern Law House, 2001.
5. Ghose, Jayanti : Seal Your Right, The Times of India 26th Nov. 2001, Vol.I No. 34 (Eduactional Times) P.1.

15

VIOLATIONS IN MUSIC INDUSTRY AND THE POLICE IN INDIA

Sridevi Goel

Introduction

Copyright is the right over one's literary property as recognized and sanctioned by law. It is intangible, incorporeal intellectual property right granted by the statute to the author or the creator of certain literary or artistic productions, whereby he is accorded for a limited period (sixty years) the sole and exclusive privilege of producing multiple copies, publishing and selling the same. It is the actual works, creations that enjoy copyright. In the case of a literary work, copyright is vested with the author of the book. If the work is done by an author for a consideration of a publisher, the copyright in it would normally vest in the publisher, contrary to S.18, the copyright could be assigned and if it is so done, it would be vested in the purchaser. In the case of a musical work, the composer is the owner of the copyright.

The oft-resorted to provisions under the Copyright Act, 957, either stand alone or in conjunction with other Acts such as Merchandise Act, IPC under its Ss.51, 52A, 63, 68(A) etc.,. Infringement of copyright relating to literary, dramatic, musical or artistic work is treated as piracy and taken cognizance of accordingly in the district court (JMFC, MM) having jurisdiction.

Section 63 is a penal section that spells out punishment of imprisonment for a term not less than 6 months but which may extend upto 3 years with fine which shall be less than 50,000 rupees but which may also extend to two lakh rupees. Section 63 also provides for enhanced punishment for second and every subsequent offence. Section 64 empowers a Police Officer, not below the rank of sub-inspector to seize without warrant all copies of the work and the plates used for the purpose of making infringement copies and produce them before the Magistrate.

Piracy menace in music in Asia

Problem of piracy has arisen with the rapid advance of technology. New techniques of printing, recording and fixation of broadcast or recorded programmes have made easy the pirate's job. While film makers leave no stone unturned to ensure that film they produce does not find it's way into the drawing rooms in India courtesy the big bad boys of the industry, video pirates and cable operators, music makers are at their wit's end. Mira Nair, the producer of the much liked film " Monsoon Wedding" hired lawyers and security agency to physically track each of the 86 prints of the movie and also secured indemnities against the leakage of prints at any point so that the security agencies and cinema house owners would repay the costs in case of a leakage. Lagaan print was leaked in transit. Pirated 'Asoka' DVDs and video cassettes of the film have been seized in Manhattan, NY in America. It's said estimated that the makers of 'ASOKA' have lost hundreds of thousands of dollars in theatre collections due to piracy since the film was released there.

Globally counterfeiting and piracy have risen to 5-7% of total world trade or above 200 to 300 billion dollar lost in revenue. According to recent estimates from the European Union most of fakes originate in Asia, where absolutely everything is counterfeited. At the top end, piracy is carried out by organized syndicates with powerful patrons in government and armed forces. According to the International Federation of the Photographic Industry one in every three recordings sold worldwide is pirated. The IFPI has been created to protect the interests of music industry worldwide. It has consultative status with world Intellectual Property Organization UNESCO and the ILO. When the Hong Kong Customs and Excise Department first began its crackdown on fake music and movie CDs in 1992, the criminal gangs moved their factories to Malaysia. An illegal optical

Disk Plant pay more than $1 million in profits every month – says an investigator " It's like winning a lottery ticket week after week". It costs around $5 million to buy machines from Germany to Taiwan that churn out more than 1 million CDs a month of music, movies, software, videogames or whatever is in demand. The pirates cover their initial outlay within three four months. After that it's cream. Each CD costs about 15 cents and it sells for around $5. However under the US Copyright Act, it will be interesting to note that there is no statutory provision for an action for contributory infringement of a copyright by providing an actual infringer with the necessary equipment or materials to make a copy of a copyright work; there the courts have recognized the existence of such a right. Any avid newspaper reader will recall the US Federal Court's decision in the Sony Corporation of America V. Universal City Studios involving the Napster Inc. Napster provides a service through which the computer users can, through the internet, download music recordings that were resident on computers of any other person who was logged on to Napster's site at the time.

Piracy in music: Picture in India

Police in India carryout reaids to detect piracy. The details of reaids carryout in India since four years are shown in table no. 1.

Cassette sales pirate recordings in 1998 were estimated at 177 million units making India the World's largest pirate market in volume and sixth in value. Pirate sales in India account for nearly 30% of total unit sales. Three kinds of illegal activities flourish in Music Industry.

1. **Counterfeiting** : Pertains to unauthorized copying of the sound, artwork, trademark, label and packaging of the original recording. The aim is to mislead the consumer into thinking they are buying the genuine product.
2. **Pirate Recordings** : These are unauthorized duplications of music from legitimate recordings for commercial gain. Pirated CDs or music cassettes sell as "Top Ten" / "Bollyhood Hits" or a combination of hit titles of different music companies.

Table No. 1. Showing Raids carried out in India

Particulars	*Years*			
	1998	*1999*	*2000*	*TillJune 2001*
No. of raids	759	947	1,054	541
Cassettes	1,213,426	5,94,486	7,69,711	2,65,597
Seized CDs seized	40,200	33,357	75,225	53,096
CCPs seized	376	292	348	174
Inlay cards Seized	3,726,437	3,253,803	3,357,879	437,459
Computers/ CD writers Seized	2	15	30	28/13
Arrests	855	1,096	1,175	584

The packaging and presentation of a pirate copy does not usually resemble a legitimate commercial release.

3. **Bootlegging :** This is the recording, duplication and sale of a performance such as live concert or broadcast without the permission of the artist or the Record Company which may be entitled to control the recording rights of the artists' performances.

Thus while pirates have nearly killed the music industry in countries like Asia, Bangladsh, Sri Lanka, the association of producers of sound recordings formed the Indian Phonographic Industry in 1936, which is now called as the Indian Music Industry – IMI. It is the premier organization working to uphold the interests of creative phonogram producers and give a sense of solidarity, purpose of and direction to various companies engaged in producing recorded music. It has members such as HMV, Universal Music, Tips, Venus, Magna Sound, BMG Crescendo, Sony Music etc. companies. The broad objectives and functions of the IMI are:

- To organize and conduct anti-piracy operations.
- To facilitate the evolution of fair trade policies and business practices.
- To promote and encourage the development of music culture.
- To liaise with government authorites on matters pertaining to the production of copyright in sound recording.

Also there is another body 'SCRIPT' i.e. Society for Copyright Regulation of Indian Producers for Films and Television, that is Registered by the Registrar of Societies, Greater Bombay, Mumbai during 1998 to protect the copyrights of cinematography films & TV films and to prevent piracy of films.

Why piracy in music industry should not be tolerated?

Piracy costs the Music Industry and the Government crores of rupees every year. It is estimated that out of nearly 4.9 crore cassettes sold each month, 1.6 crore are illegally manufactured and sold by pirates. Though not the creators of the intellectual property, the pirates evade payment of royalty, excise duty, sales tax and the promotion and publicity costs. Consumers pay for a poor quality product. Artists and other right holders are robbed of their royalties. Music companies are deprived of their rightful revenue. Government is deprived of its revenue through evasion of taxes. Piracy results in loss to the exchequer of nearly Rs. 19 crore in Sales Tax, Excise and Income Tax. It is only the pirates who stand to gain.

Government's commitments

The Ministry of Human Resource Development is responsible for copyright administration and it has set up a "Copyright Enforcement Advisory Council" to control infringement on copyrights. The Copyright Enforcement Advisory Council has advised setting up of special policy cells in the states to deal with copyright complaints.

The Berne Convention was established in 1986 in Berne, to protect international copyright through mutual co-operation. It is administrated by World Intellectual Property Organization (WIPO). The Universal Copyright Convention (UCC) was adopted in 1952 and is administrated by UNESCO. India is also a party to the Geneva Convention 1971 for protection of producer of phonograms against unauthorized duplication of their phonograms.

In the Sunil Kumar Gupta and the Petitioner - Vs - State (Respondent), Delhi High Court, 1998, the Court rightly observed that piracy affects the trade, commerce and industry of the country and thereby the economy and the revenue of the State and this will fall in the category of "economic offence". Therefore, the infringement of such intellectual property rights should be minimized by us.

How to Recognize pirated versions

Counterfeit Cassettes	Pirated Cassettes
1. Inlay cards will differ in quality and color of printing.	1. Inlay card may show poor quality print
2. Cassettes will not have the name of company on the leader tape	2. The cassette may carry a vague or unknown brand name
3. Company name will be missing on cassettes.	3. Will bear combination of titles there belonging to different companies
	4. Requirements of Sec.52 A such as name & address of the persons who have made the sound recording, & year of publication will usually be missing.
	5. A compilation of Hit Songs from different albums under names such as Top Ten, Bollywood Hits etc.

Pirated CDs

1. Source Identification code missing.
2. Point on the inlay card may be fussy and be poor quality

16

LIBRARIANSHIP, REPROGRAPHY AND COPYRIGHTS

S. P. Satarkar

Librarianship

Library is a storehouse of knowledge. Readers from different areas of society and varied requirements on different topics visit libraries. Librarianship involves acquisition, storage and retrieval of information sources. With the developments in science and technology, the information sources acquired in libraries are not limited with printed media like books and periodicals but audiovisuals, sound recordings and optical/digital/magnetic disks are also considered as information sources. Libraries acquire all such material and make them available to the users.

Considering the work of a library, it can thus be considered as a public place. It is also a service organization. Users of the library pay membership fee. Although the amount of fee collected is small, sometimes nominal and is not the only source of income, the libraries can be considered as paid services, Educational institutions are coming under the consumer acts and thus library services can also come under preview of the same.

There was a time when a university or a college library could acquire all documents published. Gradually the college and university libraries started collecting the information sources pertaining to the interested subjects only. Such subjects were the subjects in which study and teaching programs are conducted by the institution. This has resulted because of three reasons mentioned below:

1. Tremendous increase in number of documents published

2. Increase in the cost of the documents
3. Decrease in the budgetary provisions made available to libraries for purchase of documents

It is true that reader purchase information sources seldomely. Readers rely on libraries for their requirements of information sources. College students, teachers or researchers in an academic institution are not purchasing documents for their personal use. There is constant growth in the number of students undergoing higher education. Because of budgetary constraints, these libraries are not in a position to purchase sufficient number of copies of documents required by the users. Curriculum of the courses is modified every three to five years and it is essential too because of the rate of growth of knowledge. This results in requirement of new documents in sufficient number and making of some of the documents absolute. Libraries are not in good financial position so as to purchase sufficient copies of one document. Further as in higher education students are expected to go through the information sources prescribed, the demand for a particular document increases tremendously. In some cases university includes a document published 15 to 20 years ago as a text. This document would not be available in market. This results in increase in demand from the students. All these issues create problems for librarians and hamper the basic aim of librarianship given by Drury i.e. "Right information to a right reader at right time."

Reprography

Reprography is defined as production of facsimile copy.Krishnaswami,T and Krishnamurthy,R have defined the term 'Reprography" as under:

"Reprography" is a super technology with a photographic bias and has many facets under its umbrella like photography, copying and duplicating systems, micrographics, plate making systems to aid offset printing, proof making and certain pre press operations.

With the invention of xerox machines, it became much easy for a user to create and maintain a copy of required material. Reprography can be achieved as a photograph, microfilm or a xerox copy. Compared with theses three, the xerox copy preparation is much cheaper. This is one reason for encouragement in preparation of xerox copies of the document. Preparation of a photocopy is cheaper even than printing. This is second reason for its popularity. Thirdly the users could not come to the library and could not spare sufficient time to refer the document by sitting in a reading room of the library. This also increases pressure on librarians for creation of photocopies of the documents. Due to invention of reprography, librarians got relief in fulfilling the demands of the user and also for number of copies required in a library. Reprography has thus proved as a boon for the users as well as to library staff. Ultimately any libraries purchased photocopying machines, installed in the libraries and started providing photocopies to its readers at subsidized rates. Libraries do not look towards reprography facility as a profit making activity but it is given at 'No profit no loss' basis. Hence motive of this facility is service and not to earn profits. The situations mentioned above under "librarianship" show that there are sufficient grounds for providing reprography service in the libraries. University Grants Commission, New Delhi through its letter No. 1-26/2001 (CPP-II) dated August 13, 2001, has circulated the letter from the Federation of Publisher's and Book seller's Associations in India. Both the agencies have appealed to take necessary steps to stop piracy of books by the way of photocopying. Hence it is essential to look towards theses issues from the point of copyright act and the provisions there in.

Provisions in Copyright Act

Copyright is the right of holding the authority on intellectual work. Intellectual property is equally important like civil property. Copyright Act (1957) gives protection to safeguard his intellectual property. Section 51 & 52 of copyright Act (1957) amended from time to time deals with the infringements of copyright. Section 51 highlights the situations when the copyright is infringed. It states as under;

51 When copyright infringed:

Copy right in a work shall be deemed to be Infringed :

a. When any person without a license granted by the owner of the Copyright or the Registrar of Copyrights under this Act or in contravention of the Conditions of a license so granted or of any condition imposed by a Competent authority under this Act –

   I. does any thing, the exclusive right to do which is by this Act conferred upon the owner of the copyright, or

   II. permits for profit any place to be used for the performance of the work in public where such performance constitutes an infringement of the copyright in the work unless he was not aware and had not reasonable ground for believing that such performance would be an infringement of copyright, or

b. When any person

   I. makes for sale or hire, or sells or lets for hire, by way of trade Displays or offers for sale or hire, or

   II. distributes either for the purpose of trade or to such an extent as to Affect prejudicially the owner of the copyright, or

   III. by way of trade exhibits in public, or

   IV. Imports into India, any infringing copies of the work.

[Provided that nothing in sub - clause (iv) shall apply to the important of two Copies of any work, other than a cinematography film or record, for the private and domestic use of the importer.]

Provisions in this section specify that:

1. Whether the prepared copy resembles exactly to the original of not
2. Whether such copy is prepared without prior permission of the author
3. Whether such copy is prepared for use of public.

4. Motto of the preparation of such a copy is to earn profit and sale is offered
5. Innocence is no defence to a charge of infringement of copyright.

Section 52 in the in the copyright Act deals with the acts which can not be the infringement of copyright. Sub section (a), (b), (f), (g), (h), (i) are related in the present topic. It states as under: -

52. Certain acts not to be infringement of copyright

The following acts shall not constitute an infringement of copyright, namely

a. a fair dealing with a literary, dramatic, musical or artistic work for the Purposes of
   i. research or private study;
   ii. criticism or review, whether of that work or of any other work;
b. A fair dealing with a literary, dramatic, musical or artistic work for the Purposes of reporting current events,
   i. in a newspaper, magazine, or similar periodical, or
   ii. by [broadcast] or in a cinematograph film or by means of photographs;

Explanation : The publication of compilation of addresses or speeches delivered in public is not a fair dealing of such work within the meaning of this clause.

c. The reproduction of a literary, dramatic, musical or artistic work for the Purpose of judicial proceeding or for the purpose of a report of a judicial proceeding or for the purpose of a report of a judicial proceeding;
d. The reproduction of a literary, dramatic, musical or artistic work in any Work prepared by the Secretariat of a Legislature or, where the Legislature consists of two Houses, by the Secretariat of either Houses of the Legislature, exclusively for the use of the members of Legislature.

e. The reproduction of any literary, dramatic or musical work in a certified copy made of supplied in accordance with any law for the time being in force;

f. The reading or recitation in public of any reasonable extract from a Published literary or dramatic work.

g. The publication in a collection, mainly composed of non-copyright matter, bona fide intended for the use of educational institutions, and so described in the title and in any advertisement issued by or on behalf of the publisher, of short passages from published literary or dramatic works, not themselves published for the use of educational institutions, in which copyright subsists :

Provided that not more than two such passages from works by the same author are Published by the same publisher during any period of five years.

Explanation : In the case of a work of joint authorship, references, in this clause to passages from works shall include references to passages from works by any one or more of the authors of those passages or by any more of those authors in collaboration with any other person –

h. the reproduction of a literary, dramatic, musical or artistic work –

i. by a teacher or a pupil in the course of instruction; or

  I. As part of the questions to be answered in an examination; or

  II. In answer to such questions;

j. The performance, in the course of the activities of an educational

Institution, of a literary, dramatic or musical work by the staff and students of the institution, or of a cinematograph film or a record, if the audience is limited to such staff and students, the parents and guardians of the students and persons directly connected with the activities of the institution.

Considering the provisions in the act now the librarians have to decide that whether photocopy of a document is to be provided or not. The decision of the supply of photocopy is to be taken cautiously and judicially. Librarians should ask following questions to him before giving permission for printing the photocopy of a document.

1. Whether the publication is available in the market?
2. How much portion does the reader from the document ask for?
3. What is the purpose of the user who is asking for a photocopy?
4. Whether the author of the publication has died before 60 years
5. Whether the document asked is unpublished work like thesis of manuscript.
   - If answers to question Nos. 1 & 2 are positive, then photocopy should not be permitted.
   - If the purpose of the reader (Q.No.3) is research or private or study, photocopy can be permitted.
   - By asking question No. 4, librarian should verify that the minimum portion of the document should be permitted for photocopying. He should also verify that the material would be used for study only.
   - If the author of the publication has died before 60 years, the document can be photocopied but if this condition is not fulfilled, librarian must verify about authority i.e. holding the copyrights & should acquire permission from such authority.

Conclusion

Considering the issues related to the librarianship, reprography and copyrights, it can be concluded that the library authorities should permit a minimum photocopying works. This is to be done only after judicious thinking on the demand from the user. Further it should be borne in mind that the circulars issued by the Association and/or University Grants Commission will not overrule the provisions in the Copyright Act. In addition to this it can be concluded that following suggestions will be useful for improvements in this situations –

1. If a publication is out of print but prescribed for a course, libraries be permitted to prepare more than three copies of documents so as to fulfill demands of its users.
2. Cost of book production be reduced & brought to minimum, which can be equal to the cost of photocopying.
3. Libraries should not maintain & preserve photocopied documents in their libraries.
4. Minimum part of the document should be permitted if it is required to user for study purpose.
5. Photocopying of original i.e. primary information sources should not be permitted at any cost.

References

1. Arora, O. P. Ed.: The Civil Court Manual Central Acts, V. 15, Ed.12, Madras Law Journal Office,1993.
2. Krishnaswami,T. and Krishnamurthy,R.: Application of reprographic technology for print production (In Pant)-A realistic approach In Standardization in library and information work and services ,Seminar papers,35th All India Library Conference,Pune,1989.
3. Mukharjee Ajitkumar : Book Selection and Systematic Bibliography
4. Spiller David : Book Selection : An introduction to Principles and Practice

17

GREY LITERARURE AND COPYRIGHT

Pratibha A. Gokhale

Introduction

There is a continuous contribution to knowledge and exchange of ideas within scholarly communication. It is potentially global in scale and almost instantaneous in speed with fair interactivity. The powerful dynamic of the advancement in technology has shortened the life cycle of knowledge. Communication is integral to the creation of knowledge and its dissemination. Therefore tremendous importance is attached to communication - whether formal or informal. According to Artus [1], "It is the communicative process of discussion, of mutual criticism, of conjecture, refutation or acceptance, that produces scientific knowledge." Knowledge emerges out of human intellect and human intellect is the intellectual property. Human intellect manifests itself through all types of published and unpublished documents like patents, designs, trademarks, computer software and all such primary literature which contributes to existing stock of knowledge. Grey Literature or non-conventional literature has an important role in the process of generating new knowledge and hence it is a subject of Intellectual Property.

Traditional literature v/s Grey literature

The sources of information exhibit complex combination of feature. They are neither monolithic, nor homogenous but evolve from different origins. SATCOM [2] committee has reported that "Historically, informal and semiformal communications, such as personal contacts, letters, memoranda and reports with limited distribution have been the forerunners to formal publications. Their co-existence with scientific journals is established firmly on the traditions of scientific and technical communication. In comparison with formal media, the semiformal ones like preprints, technical reports, information exchange memoranda offer greater speed and flexibility in adapting communications to context."

The formal traditional literature is published in large quantity, has fairly good bibliographical control, its existence is well known and it is available through normal publication channels. The non-conventional or grey literature is usually produced in small print runs, has poor bibliographic control and not available through bookselling channels. The degree of its usefulness or its importance is not measured in terms of sale or quantity but it is based on a communication model. In the case of GL documents, what is more important is the context in which information is perceived and supplied. They offer rapid, direct and relatively cheap means of interaction than the formal publications. The formal publications also suffer from publication time lag, which is largely eliminated in GL documents.

Producers of Grey Literature

Levels and forms of production of grey literature change from one discipline to another and also from type of organization. Non-formal resources used in some fields and in some subjects can be pointed out as follows -

Fields

Academic: Institutions, Research centres	Theses, dissertation, course material, training material, lecture notes, preprints, working papers, research reports, case studies.
Industry: Business	Consultancy reports, project financing reports, safety data sheets, trade literature, house journals, manuals, application / technical notes.
Government: NGO's	All types of official publications, policy documents, circulars, committee

	reports, social survey reports, pamphlets

Subjects

Agriculture:	Bulletins, notes on higher cropping yield, diagnostic studies on crop diseases, field books, material on storage techniques
Geography:	Maps, land reports, survey reports, field reports, topological studies
Geo-Sciences:	Preprints, research reports, investigative reports, ground water data, soil surveys seismic studies, oil fields data
Medical Sciences:	Case study reports, results of clinical trials, diagnosis data, test results

This listing is neither mutually exclusive, nor collectively exhaustive, but it represents a body of knowledge available through non-formal means. The documents have their definite rôle in imparting latest information and in the total communication process. These documents provide structured and specific information - not easily obtainable anywhere else. Large percentage of information needs in developing areas is met with by GL documents, as there is progressive unfoldment of issues concerned and therefore it helps to reach conclusions. They are therefore valuable in decision support system.

Grey Literature in the networked environment

Scholarly communication in the form of grey literature in the electronic environment has created new models. Information access in the global scenario forces the professionals, researchers, businessmen to be more alert in capturing the wide spectrum of information, including traditional printed form of grey literature. All the producers of grey literature have come to view themselves as publishers. Their reports, working papers, preprints, policy statements, manuals, latest research findings, raw data on statistics - are available in networked environment for unlimited retrieval - either free of cost or as paid services. University students are encouraged to produce their accepted theses through electronic publishing via HTML/PDF formats on the university websites. The E-print archives and such publications of non-commercial websites are improving the accessibility of grey literature. Individuals and organizations have assumed the role of producers, publishers and disseminators of information through the net. The presemptive concern of the Internet users is more with access to information than its permanent retention. The non-static, dynamic nature of grey literature fits into this paradigm shift from traditional to networked environment.

Grey Literature and Copyright

Grey literature is considered as an obvious option and an immediate source of information in developing fields. When properly used, it can sharpen the organizations' status and can have an edge over another in the competitive environment. It may be stated that a source of information may have a formal status in relation to the producer. The issue of relevance and accuracy may depend largely on the reliability of the producer. The consumer of information will be the best judge in this regard.

Copyright is a form of protection provided to the authors of 'Original works of authorship." However, with GL documents, regulating the IPR laws is much more a complex problem. The law in India in this regard, does not explicitly cover grey literature. There are problems such as –

- The very existence of GL documents is largely unknown to vast majority of the user community.
- The availability and accessibility of grey literature is confined to the producers of the same.
- It is very difficult to estimate and quantify the output of GL documents in the country.
- There is no national clearing house for grey literature in India. This practice is prevalent in many countries.

- The boundary between conventional publications and grey literature is not clear.

Recommendations

There is an immediate need to establish a decentralised Information System for Grey Literature in India. The GL system, if backed by legislative act, can ensure some discipline on the part of GL producers. The present Delivery of books Act may suitably be modified to include grey literature. Definite guidelines may be prepared by an Experts' Committee to decide as to which varieties of non-conventional publications be categorised as GL documents. Different countries have a set of criteria to draw the boundaries between conventional literature, non-conventional literature and grey literature. These may be adopted suitably for this country. All non-classified grey literature in science, technology, social sciences and in developmental fields should be recorded for public knowledge. The present legal deposit laws in India apply to commercially published literature which has means to have bibliographic control. Considering the peculiar nature of grey literature, its production, non-standard methods of processing and a conservative attitude towards its dissemination - a new set of copyright laws be framed for this purpose. Ambiguities in general are likely to involve in this regard because the urge to get information from grey literature, may override the desire to protect the intellectual content - since grey literature is based on communication model rather than on economic model. Hence a great deal of work needs to be done on identification of GL documents, standardisation in their production and processing and legal laws of deposit.

Conclusion

In conclusion, it may be stated that Grey Literature as a concept is relatively new. It has a pivotal role in the information chain and with increasing globalization of information, users are likely to depend more on grey literature - whether traditional or networked, to get latest information in the given field. There may not be an immediate solution on legal issues for grey literature since it is a complex phenomena. But steps may be taken to initiate the process of including GL documents under the realms of Intellectual Property Rights. This will also enhance the utility of the otherwise hidden literature as it will receive better publicity and visibility.

References

1. Artus, M.M. - The shape of things to come? - self organizing grey literature databases for the Internet. In Proceedings of the third international conference of Grey Literature held in Luxembourg, Nov.13-14, 1997, pp.14-30.
2. Scientific and Technical Communication. A pressing national problem and recommendations for its solutions. A report by the Committee on Scientific and Technical Communication (SATCOM) of the National Academy of Sciences and Engineering, Washington D.C., 1969, p .92-93.

Section 4

Intellectual Property Rights International Scene

18

INTELLECTUAL PROPERTY RIGHTS AND COPYRIGHT : COPYRIGHT BASICS IN UNITED STATES

P. H. Barad
R.G.Kokate

Introduction

A spurt in the interest in Intellectual Property Rights (IPR) has been visible in the world for the last five years. The recent interest started with a curiosity and sometime with an element of apprehension has now graduated to a need based compulsion and desire to lay a new game introduced with the formation of World Trade Organization with the opening up to trade in goods and services the IPRs have become more important.

Intellectual property rights as a collective term include several independent intellectual property rights namely, patents copyright, trademarks, registered (Industrial) design, protection of integrated circuit design, geographical indications and protection of undisclosed information. The IPRs are awarded by the member country and most of the rights are territorial in nature, except the copyright. A copyright generated in member country of the Berne Convention is automatically protected in all the member countries, without any other property IPR can be transferred, sold or gifted.

What is Copyright?

Copyright is a form of protection provided by the laws of the United States (title 17, U. S. Code) to the authors of 'original works of authorship," including literary, dramatic musical, artistic and certain other intellectual works. This Protection is available to both published and unpublished works. As per section 106 of the 1976 Copyright Act generally gives the owner of copyright the exclusive right to do and to authorize other to do the following:

- To reproduce the work in copies or phonorecords;
- To prepare derivative works based upon the work;
- To distribute copies or phonorecords of the work to the public by sale or other transfer of ownership, or by rental, lease, or lending;
- To perform the work publicly, in the case of literary, musical dramatic, and choreographic works, pantomimes, and motion pictures and other audiovisual works;
- To display the copyrighted work publicly, in the case of literary, musical, dramatic, and choreographic works, pantomimes, and pictorial, graphic, or sculptural works, including the individual images of a motion picture or other audiovisual work; and
- In the case of sound recordings, to perform the work publicly by means of a digital audio transmission.

Who can claim Copyright

Copyright protection subsists from the time the work is created in fixed form. The copyright in the work of authorship immediately becomes the property of the author who created the work. Only the author or those deriving their rights through the author can rightfully claim copyright.

In the case of works made for hire, the employer and not the employee is considered to be the author. As per section 101 of the copyright law defines "a work made for hire" as:

- a work prepared by an employee within the space of his or her employment ; or
- a work specially ordered or commissioned for use as:
- a contribution to a collective work
- a part of a motion picture or other audiovisual work

- a translation
- a supplementary work
- a compilation
- an instructional text
- a test
- answer material for a test
- a sound recording
- an atlas

If the parties expressly agree in a written instrument signed by them that the work shall be considered a work made for hire.

The author of a joint work are co-owners of the copyright in the work, unless there is an agreement to the contrary.

Copyright in each separate contribution to a periodical or other collective work is distinct from copyright in the collective work as a whole and vests initially with the author of the contribution.

Copyright and national origin of the work

Copyright protection is available for all unpublished works, regardless of the nationality or domicile of the author.

Published works are eligible for copyright protection in the United States if any one of the following conditions is met:

- The work is first published in the United States or in a foreign nation that, on the date of first publication, is a treaty party. For purposes of this condition, a work that is published in the United States or a treaty party within 30 days after publication in a foreign nation that is not a treaty party shall be considered to be first published in the United States or such treaty party, as the case may be; or
- The work is a sound recording that was first fixed in a treaty party; or
- The Work is a pictorial, graphic, or sculptural work that is incorporated in a building or other structure, or an architectural

work that is embodied in a building and the building or structure is located in the United States or a treaty party; or

- The work is first published by the United Nations or any of its specialized agencies, or by the Organization of American States; or
- The work is a foreign work that was in the public domain in the United States prior to 1996 and its copyright was restored under the Uruguay Round Agreements Act (URAA.) Request as per Circular 38b, "Highlights of Copyright Amendments Contained in the Uruguay Round Agreements Act (URAA-GATT)," for further information.
- The work comes within the scope of a presidential proclamation.

What works are protected?

Copyright protects "original Works of authorship" that are fixed in a tangible form of expression. The fixation need not be directly perceptible so long as it may be communicated with the aid of a machine or device. Copyrightable works included the following categories:

- literary works;
- musical works, including any accompanying works
- dramatic works including any accompanying music
- pantomimes and choreographic works
- pictorial, graphic and sculptural works
- motion pictures and other audiovisual works
- sound recordings
- architectural works

What is not protected by Copyright?

Several categories of material are generally not eligible for federal copyright protection. These includes among others:

- Works that have not been fixed in a tangible form of expression (for example, choreographic works that have not been noted or recorded, or improvisational speeches or performances that have not been written or recorded)

- Titles, names, short phrases and slogans; familiar symbols or designs; mere variations of typographic ornamentation, lettering, or coloring; mere listings of ingredients or contents
- Ideas, procedures, methods, systems, processes, concepts, principles, discoveries, or devices, as distinguished from a description, explanation, or illustration
- Works consisting entirely of information that is common property and containing no original authorship (for example: standard calendars, height and weight charts, tape measures and rulers, and lists or tables taken from public documents or other common sources)

How to secure a Copyright

Copyright is secured automatically when the work is created, and a work is "created" when it is fixed in a copy or phonorecord for the first time. "Copies" are material objects from which a work can be read or visually perceived either directly or with the aid of a machine or device, such as books, manuscripts, sheet music, film, videotape, or microfilm. "Phonorecords" are material objects embodying fixations of sound (excluding, by statutory definition, motion picture soundtracks), such as cassette tapes, CDs, or LPs. Thus, for example, a song (the "work") can be fixed in sheet music ("copies") or in phonograph disks (phonorecords), or both. If a work is prepared over a period of time, the part of the work that is fixed on a particular data constitutes the created work as of that data.

References

1. Saha, R. Intellectual Property Rights & Internet, DESEDOC Bulletin of Information Technology, Vol. 20 No. 1 & 2, 2000 pp. 13 - 19.
2. Satarkar, S. P. Copyright Act & Libraries, Dnayngangotri, Nashik: YCMOU, Vol. 1, No.3, 2000 pp.25-32.
3. The Encyclopedia Britannica, 1997, Vol.3, pp. 616
4. Copyright and United State, Library of Congress home page.

19

World Intellectual Property Organisation And WIPONET

Jagdish N. Kulkarni

Introduction

The term Copyright was known from long back. Patents and trademarks were also used in one or another form. These are all related to the Intellectual product of human mind. Hence, concept of Intellectual Property covers all products produced from the human brain. This paper intends to discuss Intellectual Property rights worldwide.

Objectives

1. To introduce Intellectual Property Rights and World Intellectual Property organization.
2. To discuss development of Intellectual Property Rights under World Intellectual Property organization.
3. To highlight the activities of World Intellectual Property organization.
4. To describe WIPONET project of World Intellectual Property organization.

The word property originated from Latin word proprius means one's own. Property is an object of legal rights, which embraces possessions or wealth collectively, frequently with strong connotations of individual ownership. Intellectual property is the result from original creative thought, as patents, copyright material and trade marks. It is the ownership of something intangible. Considering this aspect the Intellectual Property is governed and protected by appropriate national legislation.

In 1873 there was an International Exhibition of Invention in Vienna. But foreign exhibitors refused to attend the exhibition because they were of the opinion that their ideas will be known to others and exploited commercially in other countries. This was first known event when the need felt for Intellectual property protection at international level.

Paris Convention was organized in the year 1886 for the protection of industrial property. It was the first major international treaty designed to help the people of one country to obtain protection in other countries for their intellectual creations in the form of industrial property rights.

Second major international event in the area of Intellectual property right was Berne convention for the Protection of Literary and Artistic Works in the year 1886. It was aimed to obtain international protection of their right to control and receive payment for their creative work. The convention set up an international bureau. It was further renamed as Bureaux for the Protection of Intellectual Property (French acronym BIRPI). It changed to World Intellectual Property Organization in 1970 and became specialized agency of United Nations Organization in the year 1974.

Objectives of the WIPO

1. To harmonize national intellectual property legislation and procedures.
2. To provide services for international applications for industrial property rights.
3. To exchange intellectual property information.
4. To provide legal and technical assistance to developing and other countries.
5. To facilitate the resolution of private intellectual property disputes and
6. To marshal information technology as a tool for storing, accessing, and using valuable intellectual property information.

WIPO is an international organization dedicated to ensure

that the rights of creators and owners of intellectual property are protected worldwide and that inventors and authors are, thus, recognized and rewarded for their work. This international protection acts as a spur to human creativity, pushing forward the boundaries of science and technology and enriching the world of literature and the arts. By providing a stable environment for the marketing of intellectual property products, it also lubricates the wheels of international trade.

The number of member states belonging to WIPO now stands at 177, over 90 per cent of the world's countries - a reflection of the crucial importance and relevance attached to the work of the Organization. With a staff of some 817 drawn from around the world, WIPO carries out many tasks related to the protection of intellectual property rights, such as administering international treaties, assisting governments, organizations and the private sector, monitoring developments in the field and harmonizing and simplifying relevant rules and practices. In all that it does, the key words are relevance, efficiency, communication and international cooperation.

A fundamental and enduring part of WIPO's activities in promoting the protection of intellectual property is the progressive development and application of international norms and standards. The Organization currently administers eleven treaties that set out internationally agreed rights and common standards for their protection, that the States which sign them agree to apply within their own territories.

While the cornerstones of WIPO's treaty system remain the Paris and Berne Conventions, subsequent treaties have widened and deepened the protection they offer, and have encompassed technological change and new areas of interest and concern. Two recent examples are the WIPO Copyright Treaty (WCT) 1996, and the WIPO Performances and Phonograms Treaty (WPPT). These treaties contain basic rules updating the international protection of copyright and related rights to the Internet age. Work is continuing on this update, for example at a Diplomatic Conference in December 2000 (Geneva) at which consensus was reached regarding most of the provisions for a proposed new treaty protecting performers (actors, musicians, etc.) against the unauthorized use of their performances in audiovisual media.

The Organization is also playing an increasing role in making industrial property registration systems more user-friendly by harmonizing and simplifying procedures. The Trademark Law Treaty (TLT) of 1994, and the Patent Law Treaty (PLT) adopted in 2000, simplify, harmonize and streamline procedures for obtaining and maintaining, respectively, a trademark and a patent in countries.

Even the most well drafted treaty is powerless without member states to bring its provisions to life, so WIPO actively encourages countries to sign its treaties and to enforce them. Widespread accession and consistent enforcement helps to maintain a stable international environment, inspire confidence that intellectual property rights will be respected around the world, encourage investment, and contribute to economic development and social well-being.

Widespread accession and consistent enforcement help maintain a stable international environment, inspire confidence that intellectual property rights will be respected around the world, encourage investment, and contribute to economic development and social well being.

WIPO also initiated a new policy to adapt to rapid changes in the field of industrial property, by using new options to speed up the development of internationally harmonized principles and rules. The adoption of international recommendations on the protection of well-known marks in 1999 and on trademark licenses in 2000 complements the traditional and lengthier treaty-based approach to international legal standard setting.

Services

The services provided by WIPO under different treaties simplify and reduce the cost of making individual applications or filings in all the countries in which protection for a given intellectual property right is sought. Some of the major services provided through treaty and directly by WIPO are,

1. Patent Cooperation Treaty
2. Impact Project
3. Madrid and Hague Systems
4. Classification of Industrial Property
5. Training and Education
6. WIPONET

World Intellectual Property Right Organization Network:

Intellectual property is becoming key issue in economic development. It is necessary to have worldwide network with the organization, which are engaged in the protection of Intellectual Property Rights. The network will help in the process of generation, valuation, protection, and exploitation of Intellectual Property. Considering changing scenario World Intellectual Property Organization has taken a decision to create a worldwide network. The decision was taken in its budget meeting on 21 January 1998.

Objectives of the WIPONET

1. To provide the necessary network infrastructure and services for improved information exchange among the global intellectual property community.
2. To derive practical benefits of the Information Technology so as to address the problem being faced in IPR administration by the member states and the IP community.

Further Standing Committee of Information Technology (SCIT) provided goals of the WIPONET as follows;

1. To narrow the information access gap that exists between the developed and developing countries.
2. To improve the flow of information concerning IPR and WIPO member states, regional Intellectual Property offices and Intellectual Bureau;
3. To improve access to and exchange of intellectual property information in terms of costs and access time in accordance with the agreed upon principles;

4. To improve intellectual property information dissemination.
5. To consider information needs and filing requirements of applicants and develop electronic services, keeping in the mind the need to provide benefits to applicants and IP offices and to other interested circles;
6. To help guide IP to cope up with information technologies; and
7. To improve the retrieval of intellectual property information through further development of international classification of patents, trademarks and industrial designs as efficient search tools.

The WIPONET is a global information network. It is the first step in enhancing communication between WIPO and the Intellectual property community. It will interconnect 332 intellectual property offices in 171 countries. The basic services which WIPONET provides are email, list services, web hosting, file transfer services, discussion groups on Intellectual Property related topics, virus scanning and the provision of updated signatures and use administration. It also provides portal like Intellectual property digital libraries (IPDLs) and on line filing under the patent cooperation treaty.

The WIPONET project will be completed in two phases. First phase will focus on setting up the project's infrastructure at the WIPO International Bureau in Geneva, establishing basic connectivity for those member states with no Internet access and providing basic services to the whole IP community. Sixty-four countries will be covered under first phase and remaining countries will be covered under second phase.

A Web site is established on Internet, which provides all information on WIPO. WIPO worldwide academy provides distance education through Internet. There are special courses for awareness and depth study in IPR.

WIPO also has developed Arbitration and mediation center that helps for setting commercial disputes related to IPR. It is a quick and inexpensive way for setting commercial disputes. A complain can be filed using model documents made available on the web site (www.WIPO.org) designed under WIPONET project. The entire procedure is conducted on line resulting in enforceable decisions within two months. WIPONET will also provide help desk in six languages, which will be for twenty-four hours without any break.

The WIPO and WIPONET really are the "Kalpvriksh" where you will get every thing about IPR.

References

1. Mashelkar, R. A.: The role of WIPONET in the development and transter of technology and its contribution to the modernization of Intellectual Property services, *Information today and tomorrow*, Vol. 19, No. 2, PP.1-6, 30.
2. *www.WIPO.org*
3. Gupta, V.K.: Basic concepts of IPRs and their management in R.&D, Chemical Industry News XL (9), 1995, pp. 1131-1135.

20

PUBLIC LENDING RIGHT : AN INTEGRAL PART OF COPY RIGHT

Vijaya Rajhansa

The Public Lending Right (PLR) can no longer is treated as a marginal experiment. In various forms it now covers nearly half of Public Library lending in the Western World. Denmark was the first country to have it since 1946 while the British Scheme dates back to 1982, which uses computer technology and statistical sampling to make very precise calculations of book issues.

PLR is essentially a payment for the author, which is based on the number of his or her books held by any given Library and an annual sampling of loans of the author's books to the general public. In other words some PLR programmes reward authors on the basis of circulation of their books in a sample of libraries, while other programmes reward authors on the extent to which copies are held in libraries. The former schemes tend to benefit best selling authors, the latter are deemed better for beginning or specialised authors. The issue is whether author's potential income is really affected by the presence of his works in the libraries or by circulation from them. The matter being discussed is whether the presence of a book in a library results in the patron borrowing it instead of buying it. Alternatively people think that a library's possession of a book publicises it and results in additional sales by book-oriented people, and thus fetches more royalty to authors.

PLR became a controversial issue when many of its proponents compared it, as a concept, with copyright and royalty payment. They advocated that PLR Legislation should be an integral part of the Copyright Law. Opponents believe that PLR is best suited for a separate piece of legislation.

What is Public Lending Right (PLR)?

PLR is a subsidy paid to authors in respect of books issued from public libraries. PLR was described by John W. Sumison in simple words as follows:

Authors earn their living by royalties on each copy of the book sold. When their books are borrowed from public libraries the result is unfair to writers; since there is only a single royalty but dozens of readers read the book. In democratic tradition free reading has acquired prominent place in any society. Most of the people, who read books after their formal education is completed, do not buy them. They borrow books free of charge from libraries. This democratic tradition has ignored the fact that author also has a right: a right to be paid for the use of his books in public libraries. In general it was felt that it is a social unfair to allow a book still in copyright to be borrowed from a public library (either free or on payment) without payment of any kind to the living author. To correct this unfairness, government gives money to authors in proportion to the number of times their books are borrowed in public libraries.

History of the PLR

In Scandinavian Countries the PLR schemes were in existence in Denmark (1946), Norway (1947), Sweden (1954), and Finland (1964), and in Sweden the Swedish Author's Fund was in existence nearly for a decade before the scheme formally came into existence in 1954.

The proposal that authors should be remunerated for the multiple use of their works in libraries was discussed in U.K. prior to the Second World War. But in 1950s idea of PLR was debated in U.K. In 1951 an effective campaign was launched by John Brophy, a novelist, who proposed that one penny (later on called as the 'Brophy's Penny' or 'Penny Levy') should be paid by each reader in respect of each book borrowed) [3]. The issuing library would collect the pennies, deduct 10% for administrative charges and hand over the balance money to publishers for transmission to their authors. There was a big debate over the issue, but Government did not take up the matter.

During the period 1951 to 1979, public libraries in UK developed to a great extent and this development coincided with the demise of subscription libraries. There was tremendous growth in the free lending of books from public libraries as well as the huge expansion of paperbacks. Due to these factors PLR became a vital issue for British writers, since lending activity of public libraries in Britain is high at 11.2 annual issues per capita. Fiction represents 60% and children's books represent 18% of total national lending. One third of books being read come from public library. About 7% of publishers' home sales are to public libraries [(4)].

In 1960 Society of Authors in U.K., under the leadership of Sir Alan Herbert, proposed an amendment to the Copyright Act, 1956, which would have had the effect of incorporating Public Lending into the activities controlled under copyright legislation. Sir Alan Herbert [(5)] has pointed out that 'Indeed the larger the country, the greater the damage' to authors by way of loss of money. He continued to make some unsuccessful attempts to amend the Public Libraries and Museums Bill during 1964 too. By 1970s a Writers' Group led by Brigid Brophy and Maneen Daffy was active.

In 1971 Jack Dove [(6)] presented his view that Library Association should take active part in discussion on PLR, which was a subject of vital concern to every public librarian. In the same year Lord Eccles, the then Paymaster General, set up a Working Party to consider how an amendment to the Copyright Act, 1956, which added 'lending to the public' to the acts restricted by copyright, might be implemented. The Working Party's report was published in 1972, however, due to inherent difficulties no legislation arose from the report. Richard Combs [(7)] supported John Brophy's view that almost everyone connected with the publishing business makes a living at it, except the writers, without whom the trade would not begin to exist.

In 1974 a Private Member's Bill was introduced by Mr. Erle Money to amend the Copyright Act, 1956. Although the Bill received substantial support in the House, due to lack of time could not receive a second reading.

In 1975 Mr. W.H.G. Harvey [8] presented to Mr. Hugh Jenkins the Minister for the Arts, 'PLR: the final report of an investigation of technical and cost aspects', which attempted to identify all major practical problems and proposed suggestions to overcome them.

In 1976 Canadian Library Association [9] at its Annual General Meeting strongly urged the Federal Government to develop and fund a system of increased financial rewards to writers including the administrative costs of such a system and indicated its readiness to supply the data of library holdings use in recognition of the cultural importance of the contributions of Canadian Writers.

Paul Whitney [10] at IFLA's Annual General Conference held at Jerusalem, in August 2000, reviewed the current status of PLR in Commonwealth Countries, where New Zealand introduced PLR first in 1973, Australia in 1974, the U.K. in 1979, Canada in 1986, Mauritius in 1999. New Zealand bases PLR payments on holdings and not circulation. Germany and Australia compensate to publishers as well as authors. Australia makes payments to foreign-based Australian citizens and resident foreign nationals as well. Australia has recently announced an Educational Lending Right, which means the payments will be made to authors whose works are being held in school, college and university libraries and lent out to students and teachers. Canada also makes payments based on holdings in public and university libraries. But, as in Israel, 'How to do' type books and textbooks are excluded from the PLR scheme.

In U.K. the PLR programme has been functional since 1979 and payments are based on public library loans and importance of popular fiction in public library circulation is noticed prominently. The payment per loan has not varied. The Government has announced a significant 40% increase in funds from 2002 and additional 7.2% in 2003-4. However, many writers have received reduced payment as a direct result of declining circulation in U.K. public libraries.

The PLR scheme operation

The main PLR operation which began in 1982 in U.K. involves the following four main steps:

1. **Author Registration :** Authors living in the U.K. can only register the books and no books can be registered for authors who died before 1982. The authors have to apply for their books to be placed on Register. The right is established by registration and is distinct from Copyright. As an Intellectual Property Right, it can be assigned or bequeathed. Each edition is registered separately and joint authors, translators, editors, compilers, illustrators have to make an agreement about their percentage of share in the amount that is being paid by the Government to the author.
2. **Loans Estimates :** Statistical sampling is employed to estimate the annual issues of all books borrowed from select twenty U.K. public libraries. Libraries issue their books with electronic computer (light pen) equipment to read special bar code labels in the books. Hence maintaining record of issue statistics is comparatively an easy job. Some 36% of loans relate to books registered and count for payment. But the PLR statistics takes care of only home lending activity of libraries and ignores the duration of loan period, whether it is one week or one month. It also excludes use of general and reference collection consulted in the library premises.
3. **Payment Calculations :** The PLR computer tallies these national loan estimates against the Register. After huge calculations and dividing the available Government annual grant of £2,403,000, estimates of payments to be made to each author for each of his registered book is given. Every author gets a computerised statement of calculations for all his registered books and nearly 1.02 Pence per loan. Many authors have been pleasantly surprised to note from the computerised statement as to how popular they are and how many of their books are being read by members of public libraries. Sometimes the books published in early fifties are out of print, yet author receives payment for them due to their current circulation, if they are registered with PLR Scheme.

4. **Financial Funding :** All the costs of the scheme are met from Central Government funding. From Government money the operating costs and library expenses are first deducted and the balance amount is distributed among authors..

During first decade of PLR working, the suspicions of the librarians were confirmed that it does little or nothing for the vast majority of authors of modest standing. It only adds to the income of the already well-off, best-selling writers. In 1990-91 less than 100 authors received £6000/-, the maximum payment, whereas more than 11,600 writers received less than £100/- [11] .

Conclusion

There are two sides of the PLR coin. On one side there is question of legal concept. Is there an author's right? How does it relate to existing copyright legislation? Graham P. Cornish[12] Confirms that connection between PLR and Copyright was not true until the introduction of the Lending/Rental legislation of 1988./ However, under this act lending and rental of certain materials became an exclusive right of the Copyright owner. Since 1996 this right has been extended to all materials which indicates that PLR and Copyright are now firmly linked. The legal status of PLR as a new property right may be more important in years to come and further debates on PLR may throw light on the unresolved problems of photocopying, musical recording, database downloading, etc..

Another issue being discussed is `Can PLR be compared with performing right?' In general the ordinary man feels that there is real case for something to be done to deal with the inequity of writers getting only one royalty, when his book is sold to a public library and then read by dozens of readers. The remuneration of an artist (singing on radio) and author (writing book) reflects changes in the media and PLR does reflect this change of medium. No one argues against musician's right to some income for his radio performance. Public library lending is a similar use and PLR takes care of the payment which author should receive for the same.

Wherever PLR is in place, it is highly valued by authors, not only for the financial remuneration, but for the fact that PLR serves to affirm the life of books long after their commercial span is over; and in present times as the commercial life span shortens, PLR becomes more important. PLR is evolving in countries where it is already existing and there are positive signs that it will spread to new areas in the near future.

References

1. Harrod's Librarians' Glossary' Hants Gower Publ. Co., 1995, p. 522.
2. Sumison, John, W.: Public Lending Right : an appraisal. Library Association Record. Vol.88, No.2, Feb. 1988, p.71.
3. Taylor, L.J.: A Librarian's handbook. London, Library Association, 1976, p. 397.
4. Sumison, John W. : Public Lending Right: the U.K. experience. Journal of Library & Information Science, Vol. 13, No.1, June p. 85.
5. Harrison, J. Clement : Another battle of the books. Library Journal, Vol.88, No.10, May 15, 1963, p. 1948.
6. Dove, Jack : A Librarian's view. In P.L.R.: a matter of justice; ed. By Richard Findlater, London, Andre Deutsch, 1971, p. 75.
7. Combs, Richard : Public Lending Rights and wrongs, Wilson library Bulletin, Vol.47, N0.2, December 1972, p. 354.
8. Harvey, W.H.G.: PLR : final report of an investigation of technical and cost effects. London, H.M.S.O. 1975, p. 1.
9. Ellsworth, Rudolph C.: Library royalties in Canada : a status report Libri, Vol. 27, No.3, p. 200-201.
10. Whitney, Paul : P.L.R. in Commonwealth Countries www. Ifla.Org.
11. World Encyclopedia of Library and Information Services 3rd ed. Chicago, Ame. Lib Association, 1993 p. 838.
12. Cornish, Graham : Copyright : interpreting the law for libraries, Archives and information services : 3rd rev. ed. London, Library Association, 2001, p. 90, p. 167.

21

A Focus On Intellectual Property Rights And Biotechnology

G. Gyananath

The rapid developments in biotechnology in areas like food, agriculture, industrial products, medicinal treatment, environmental cleanup, health care etc. have produced tangible results more quickly than traditional means. The advances in biological research particularly in the area of biotechnology has generated interest and debates on contentious issues such as cloning, biopiracy, biosafety, germline engineering, genetically modified foods, genetic piracy and discrimination, DNA banking, Life patents , Xenotransplantation etc. As a consequence, the impact of biotechnology created public awareness in a variety of sectors like agriculture, environment, pharmaceuticals and medicine etc.

Legal status

The Intellectual Property Rights (IPR) are legal instruments which confer protection on processes or products of research and development efforts and formally assure the allocation of benefits to the innovator in return for full disclosure to society. The different forms of IPR that confer protection include patents, copyrights, trademarks, designs etc. of these, patents are most important form of protection for R&D organizations particularly in biotechnology. Patents are granted as inventions which are novel, inventive, with a useful application and sufficiently described to allow verification. The disclosure can stimulate further research and the knowledge can be shared by others with the inventor. Patents are of national origin and are enforceable in the country which grants the permit for a period of 17 to 20 years.

The role and importance of IPR and biotechnology in developing countries has not been adequately addressed either due to lack of practitioners in this discipline or the scope of protection has not been adequately defined for implementation. Although many developing countries have established detailed legislation and rules in this regard, it is important for developing countries to create significant data base that meets the requirements of World Trade Organization (WTO) and Trade Related Intellectual Property Rights (TRIPs). Some of the concerns like biodiversity protection, food security, health and economy in addition to ethical and religious concern, equity consideration etc can be ensured through IP protection and patent protection.

International scene of Biotechnological rights

A fundamental change in the 1990's as a consequence of molecular revolution launched over 42 years ago with the discovery of DNA transformed the structure of industry. A large number of industries particularly from the pharmaceuticals have utilized the scientific advances in genetics and molecular biology to design and manufacture synthetic drugs. The lead role by the American Pharmaceutical industry not only resulted in the resurgence of trading system but also provided a competitive edge in the world markets. Under the WTO and TRIPs, India is entering the arena of Intellectual property Protection of international standards. Under the GATT, all member countries must bring their national IPR laws into conformity with the provisions of the new agreement on TRIPS. The establishment of TRIPs ensures minimum standards for enforcement and protection of IPR to patent system in both developed and developing countries.

The U.S. has one of the more well developed patent systems in terms of patent law and case history, particularly in the area of pharmaceuticals (McCarthy, 1995). Patents have been issued to companies from developed countries particularly for pharmaceuticals and cosmetic purposes. Over 100 countries allow some patent protection, but developing countries often include exclusions for pharmaceuticals and agricultural inputs. India has denied patents altogether in the field of pharmaceuticals and agricultural products on grounds that these products are essential for the public welfare.

The Argentines have used their IPR laws in to conformity with the TRIPS. They have their IPR laws to develop a strong pharmaceutical sector that has contributed to its national economy and become a powerful competitor in the global market place. In both Argentina and Brazil, their congresses have also fought against altering their national laws to conform to the TRIPs.

Till recently, patents are restricted to inanimate inventions such as new engines, vacuum cleaners, drugs, or processes for producing chemicals. The first patent was awarded in the USA in 1980 for a microorganism that could degrade oil and which was further extended to higher plants and animals in USA and Europe.

The Convention on Biological Diversity (CBD) establishes sovereignty and right to control access to genetic resources and biodiversity. It promotes the sharing of benefits that derived from the use of genetic resources/ or biodiversity in areas such as pharmaceuticals and biotechnology. The CBD establishes important principles regarding the protection of biodiversity while recognizing the commercial value of germplasm. Until the CBD, living organisms was regarded as the common heritage of mankind and in 1983, countries recognized that plant resources were part of the common heritage of mankind and should be respected without any restriction.

The developments in modern agriculture biotechnology requires the use of several processes and products, which in most cases will be subject to plant protection (e.g. Genetically Modified Crops). But the lack of appropriate mechanisms for sharing the benefits has generated considerable controversies. A much cited example is that of the neem tree and basmati rice that have gone through legal battle . Common food items like Brinjal (Solanum melangena), Bitter gourd (Syzinnum lumini), and jamun (Monodica charantia) have entered into controversy over patent rights. The Department of science and Technology is considering for challenging the granting of patents plants that have been traditionally used as medicine through the food (The Hindu, 1999 I).

In 1961, the Convention on the International Union for the Protection of New Varieties of Plants (UPOV Convention) established

Plant Variety Rights and by 1989 there were 19 member countries, which include more than 70% of the world seed market of all countries with a market economy. Some countries in Africa support the UPOV convention while some developing countries show mixed reception to IP and others want to restrict the overall patenting of plant varieties.

Plant Varieties Protection (PVP) provides protection to new plant varieties that have not been previously commercialized, that are distinct from existing varieties, that are uniform in their characteristics and stable over the years for those characteristics. PVP has been ratified by 44 countries including a number of developing countries. The patenting of new varieties of plants and animals is subject to some restriction in some countries but internationally the concept of farmers rights are accepted under the CGFRA, and the CBD. A new flower pattern can be patented, and a new property can be patented but a whole flower cannot. Sexually reproducing varieties cannot be patented but can be protected under the PVP Act of 1970 (McCarthy,1995).

There has been no protection to plant varieties in India so far. The Indian law granted only process patents and no product patents in pharmaceutical and agrochemicals. The patent protection for pharmaceuticals and agrochemicals in India is based on reverse engineering because the country is yet to modify 35 acts for implementation before 1st January, 2005 in line with the requirements under TRIPS. The products of pharmaceuticals and agrochemicals are eligible for patent protection after 1st January, 2005 and that protection will be for a specific period of time. The parliament has just passed the protection of plant varieties and farmer's bill, 2000. It will soon become a law.

Genetics and IPR

The question of patenting genetic material continues to be a contentious issue despite the global agreement within Article (4) of the Universal Declaration on the Human Genome and Human Rights passed by the General Assembly in 1997, and adopted by the UN General Assembly in 1998 which states that ' The human genome in its natural state shall not give rise to financial gain'. Therefore, it is suggested that living organisms and their genetic material should be considered as special and different to other materials. In the UK, patenting of genetic material shall not be granted for an invention. Similar exclusions are common to European and US patent laws. France and Japan have opposed to such patents.

Biopiracy of genetic resources is one of the controversial areas of genomics research. The lack of property rights for genetic resources or its poor definition is one of the major factors hindering the valuation of genetic resources. The search for useful genes – 'bioprospecting' in developing countries is high as these countries contain much of the world's biodiversity and companies have to find compounds they can use as drugs or genes that can help in new crop developments. The isolation of a gene from its natural environment and the identification of its function render the gene and its sequence an invention for patenting purposes in some countries. There is less support for patenting genes or living organisms but there is support for patenting a cure for AIDS. Recent developments in AIDS treatment give us all hope for helping those already living with HIV and for preventing new infections by interrupting maternal to child transmission. A modern patent system helps promote the rapid innovation, development, and commercialization of effective and safe drug therapies against HIV/AIDS.

In 1991 and 1992, patent applications for nearly 3000 human genes based on randomly sequenced cDNAs were made by the National Institutes of Health in the USA. In 1999, the Helix Research Institute of Japan applied for a patent on 6000 human genes, similar to the US Genomics companies that has applied for patents on many genes. These raised major questions about patenting policy because researchers are reluctant to share genetic sequence data in databases while there is the possibility of others abusing it, and when the NIH and MRC have withheld their data from entry into gene databases while preparing patent applications.

Recent attempts to patent DNA sequences with unknown functions, human cell lines, and transgenic animals have accelerated the controversy over identifying true contributors to an invention (Gross and Carey, 1996). Denmark has exclusion in its national law to patenting of animals, and the Nigerian patent law of 1970 excluded biological products and processes. This exclusion is based on ethical arguments. Since the animals need to be reproduced by biological process, reproduction, they can be regarded as patentable. In 1999, a new patent directive by the European Commission effectively allowed the patenting of transgenic organisms. The production of transgenic animals and plants and the intense resistance to altered foods and animal products by European and Asian consumers has European and Canadian Governments to ban foods having any transgenic components. The National Wildlife Foundation opposes patenting for transgenic animals because of the lack of legislation in the area concerning their release into the wild and allowing the patents will cause a greater number of transgenic animals to be created, thus increasing the risk to the environment.

Methods for gene sequencing, or mapping, or expression, can be invented or patented. The information may be used in the study of a particular disease, for example by the introduction of a gene into an animal to make a model for a particular disease. The process of making 'Oncomouse', a mouse that contains activated oncogene sequences that is sensitive to carcinogens, was patented., and it was the first mammal to be patented, in 1988 in the USA. The genetic information can be used to cure a disease, for example using the technique of gene therapy with a specific gene vector. The use of automated DNA sequencers is not considered as innovative technology and the publication of such sequence markers will make it more difficult for companies to patent those genes. The UK Government is in the process of amending UK law to explicitly allow the patenting of genes, cells, plants and animals. According to UK patent office, Government is funding bioprospecting projects for plants, fungi and insects in partnership with pharmaceutical companies. India, has been a special target for bioprospectors.

Conclusion

One of the important developments in the genome project is the completion of genome sequencing several years ahead of schedule, in the year 2000, instead of 2005. This resulted in competition among major pharmaceutical companies in the development of Single Nucleotide polymorphisms (SNPs) maps which allows companies to explore individual SNPs for medical treatment. The issue being commercialization of biotechnology is an attempt that allows companies to patent as many SNPs so that the claims can be listed in the public domain. Although, much effort has been invested for harmonization of patent laws by different countries as a result of NAFTA and GATT much remains to be done as it is not possible for a single country to stand on its own in a changing global system. In order to ensure that the WTO agreement on TRIPS are respected, the agreement takes special note of the least developed countries to grant time limited exclusive rights through patents until 2006.

References

1. Intellectual Property Rights Protection: An overview Fact Sheet. U. S. Department of State. *http://usinfo.state.gov/topical/econ/ipr/ipr-overview.htm*
2. Electronic forum on biotechnology in food and agriculture. http://www.fao.org/biotech/C6 doc.htm
3. International policy on Plant genetic Engineering Michelle Thom http://www.rz.uni-frankfurt.de/ecstein/gen/iatp/ipr-info 11.html
4. Gene watch, UK No 11, June 2000.
5. Role of IPR in biotechnology transfer – corporate views W. Lesser Prepared under WIPO special service agreement.
6. IPR and Health policy *http://usinfo.state.gov/topical/econ/ipr/ipr-overview.htm*
7. IPR and biodiversity Kristin Dawkins, Michelle Thom and Carolyn Carr. http://www.rz.uni-frankfurt.de/ecstein/gen/iatp/ipr-info 11.html
8. IPR in the WTO: Major issue in the millennium around Sylvia Ostry Fraser Institute Conference, Santiago Chile, April 19, 1999.
9. Inventions, patents and Moralit Institute of biological sciences, University of Tsukuba, Japan. Encyclopaedia of Life Support Systems (UNESCO 2001).
10. Intellectual property Rights Issues – Industry Perspective VR Kaundinya, Mahendra Hybrid Seed Co., Hyderabad, Workshop on Intellectual property Rights in Biotechnology, CCMB, October ,2001.

22

Intellectual Property Rights In Agriculture

V. K. Gupta

Introduction

The Indian Council of Agricultural Research (ICAR), the research arm of the Ministry of Agriculture, and the network of agricultural universities across the country constitute the main infrastructure of the National Agricultural Research System (NARS). ICAR performs a variety of functions including determination of national research policies and priorities, linking them with government's development objectives and establishing and managing a large network of research institutes and centers. Its diverse institutions cover agricultural research in its wide sense including crops, veterinary and animal science, fisheries, agro-forestry, soil science, agricultural engineering and post harvest technology, socio-economic and other related disciplines.

ICAR is in the forefront of guiding the change and re-orientating research in commensurate with the new transformations in economic policies and reforms. The quintessence of these transformations in the economic competition and ensuring the household food and nutrition security in the country. Two most important tasks in the overall strategy of reorientation of research are to enhance productivity and profitability while ensuring protection of the natural resource base as well as sustainability of agriculture. As a result, the research needs are to be focused on areas of clear comparative advantages. This may require a shift in the emphasis from commodity research towards production system research, increasing emphasis on sustainability of production system as practised by farmers by adopting systematic co-ordination on cross-cutting issues such as land and water management, integrated pest management etc.

The new agricultural research system would need to address the issues of excellence in basic and strategic research, the location specific technology generation and potential for wider applicability with greater probability of success. The contribution of knowledge is of central importance in this context. For example, the need for moving upstream in frontier technologies like biotechnology, informatics, environmental science, geographic information system, computer science etc. is well recognized.

Intellectual Property

Intellectual property rights (IPRs) are granted to reward creativity. From societal point of view, IPRs strive to balance the private interests of creators, by ensuring that they have an incentive to create, against those of the society at large in having the information available for their use. Eventhough information does not diminish once it is shared, the role of IPRs is to ensure that information providers do not lose rights to the information by disclosing it, Since such information can be used by a number of persons simultaneously. Society gains by getting access to the inventive process and product, which can be used by other inventors for making improvements as well as developing substantive new innovations. Inventor benefits by having incentive to invest or assign it to some one else interested in commercial exploitation of the invention. The main elements of intellectual property are copyrights and related rights, trademarks, geographical indications, industrial designs, patents, layout designs (topographies) of integrated circuits, protection of undisclosed information, and the control of anti-competitive practices in contractual licenses. The IPR laws in India have been reserved or are under revision in light of the commitments under TRIPS.

The initiatives to amend its patent laws according to the commitments of TRIPS have been taken in two phases. In the first amendment act of 1999, the provisions for filing product patents and the grant of exclusive marketing rights (EMR) for five years from the data of such grant for product patents filed after January 1, 1995 were introduced. In the second phase, based on broad-based consultations, the Government introduced the second amendment bill in the parliament on December 20, 1999. The bill was referred to the selected Parliamentary Committee and is still under its consideration.

The Copyright Act has since been amended in 1999 in line with latest development at the international levels providing for protection of software, database, and broadcasting, reproduction right and the performer's right. The Trade and Merchandise Marks Act of 1958 was replaced by a new Trademarks act in 1999, keeping in view the changes in trade and commercial Practices, and the need for simplification and harmonization to trade marks registration systems. A New act called the Geographical Indication of Goods (Registration and Protection) Act, 1999 has been put in place. The earlier legislation on industrial designs was replaced by a new legislation, namely, the Designs Act in 2000, which introduced a more detailed classification of design to conform to the international system. The legislation conformed to international trends in design administration. The Semiconductor Integrated Circuits Layout Designs Act was passed in 2000 recently, the plant Variety Protection and Farmers' Right Act has been cleared by the Parliament for enforcement.

India participates in many bilateral arrangements or multilateral international treaties and conventions concerning intellectual property rights, which have bearing upon the nature of amendments in her national laws. For example, India is an active member of World Intellectual Property Organization (WIPO), Paris Convention for the Protection of Industrial Property, Patent Cooperation Treaty, Berne Convention, Universal Copyright Convention, Trademark Law Treaty on Intellectual Property in Respect of Integrated Circuits, International Convention of Biological Diversity, Copyright Treaty and the phonogram and Performers Rights Treaty of 1996, the commitments under all of which have required appropriate adjustments in national laws. More importantly, India's Joining of the World Trade Organisation (WTO), and the Agreement on Trade Related Aspects of Intellectual Property Rights (TRIPS) on first January 1995 prompted all together new dimensions in its intellectual property regime.

Plant Variety Protection

Intellectual Property rights (IPRs) and plant breeding has, historically, had nothing to do with each other. In India and many other developing countries, patents were never allowed on life forms because of ethics, the provisions of the national patent laws and the threat that statutory monopolies in the health and food sectors pose to peoples, basic needs. Unlike manufactured products, biological material was considered the realm of nature and therefore regarded as a "discovery " not an invention. Agriculture was also not subjected to patents. This was linked to traditional agricultural practices of seed saving and exchange and to the perception that the fulfillment of food needs should not primarily be a profit –making enterprise. With the developments in the hybrid seed industry and, later the biotechnology-driven life sciences industry plant breeding has become big business and those businesses wanted exclusive rights to the research results. In response, the instruments of plant variety protection (PVP) were developed for the protection of new crop varieties so as to provide incentives to breeders to innovate and disclose the improvements. Laws of PVP were gradually attuned to the needs of agriculture. It guaranteed breeders a commercial monopoly on the use of their varieties while leaving certain options open for farmers and other breeders.

Plant variety protection is synonymous with plant breeder's rights (PBRs). PBRs and patents are based on similar premises in so far as they both seek to give incentives to inventors enter a particular industry. PBRs provide a form of legal protection for plant varieties different from patents and are less stringent. The main difference between PBRs and patents is that the scope of protection of the former is more limited. At the same time, PBRs are designed to allow plant breeders to use the4 protected plant for their own breeding activities and research as long as they refrain from selling the protected plant itself. Further, new varieties derived from such breeding activities can be marketed.

Farmers' Rights

The farmers' rights include the rights to produce one's crop and use product of crop as seeds for further crop. The rights ensure the equitable sharing of benefits arising from genetic resources and give farmers incentives of preserve genetic resources. The most recent articulation of farmers' rights focuses on the protection of traditional knowledge, the equitable sharing of benefits arising from the exploitation of biological resources and the right to participate in decision-making.

Indian Plant Variety and Farmers' Right Bill (PVFRB), 1999

The Indian government has preferred to use sue generic system instead of patents for the protection of plant varieties. The bill provides flexibility, better protection of farmers' rights and stronger exemptions for researchers to use the protected varieties for research purposes. The bill provides for the setting up of gene fund, which will determine the share of benefits to be given to farmers or other breeders and also decide the eligibility for getting benefits, whether benefits are given one time or on recurrent basis. There is a provision for registration of extant varieties, i.e. the ones notified under Seed Act, 1966 released by the Central Seed Committee. The provision also exists for preservation jointly or severally of wild species or a traditional variety with or without added value and which has economic use.

The farmer's rights include the right to produce his crop, use product of crop as seeds for producing further crop, and sell product of crop except its sale exposing it as a seed. The distinctiveness of the variety is defined by its distinguishability by at least one essential characteristic from and other variety whose existence is a matter of common knowledge in and country at the time of filing of filing of application. Failure of and application for the grant of breeders right to a new variety or its derivatives shall seemed to render that variety as matter of common knowledge. The applicant is required to provide complete data of the parent line from which new variety or its propagating material has been developed.

The bill provides for the Researchers Right under which an authorization of breeder of plant variety protection holder is necessary when repeated use of parental lines of a variety is required. Otherwise nothing will prevent any researcher from using a protected variety as a research material. The farmers have the right to save, use exchange, share or sell his farm produce of a protected variety except when covered by contractual market arrangement.

The bill provides for the option of compulsory licensing when reasonable quantity of seed or reproductive material of protected variety is not made available in the country. The Government has the power to determine which genra and species would be covered under the plant variety protection. In case have and disputes regarding orders of Indian PVFRB Authority, the high courts will have the jurisdiction for resolving any complaints. There is a provision for non- registration of the varieties, which are injurious to the public morality or health as in the case of "terminator gene."

The rights of communities stipulate that the people of any community or an NGO representing them can represent the contribution of people to a variety granted protection. The Indian plant variety and farmer's right bill has unique features such as opportunity for registration of extant varieties, registration of farmer's traditional varieties by communities of NGOs on their behalf, and constitution of National Gene Fund.

Traditional Knowledge

Traditional knowledge is the product of the continuity of creative skills and craftsmanship in a variety of cultures, traditions and beliefs since ancient period. The knowledge and ideas have flown freely across cultures and gained strength from the interactions amongst civilizations. Apart from the rich bio-diversity resources, the traditional societies have generated a vast reservoir of information and experiences that have help in sustaining their social and economic life. India possesses a great wealth of biological diversity in its forests, its wetlands and in its marine areas. Its species of flowering plants range up to 15,000 as compared to 25,000 species in the world. In addition, there are more than four thousand different species of animal kingdom against about 45,000 species at the world level.

According to Pushpangadan and Nair, the systematists have identified, catalogued and classified about 1,26,565 species of plants, animals, fungi and microorganisms from different bio-geographic zones of India. There is still a lot more to be explored and documented.

The world Intellectual Property Organization has been exploring the role of intellectual property protection in the context of traditional knowledge. The issues are far from being clear and require greater technical understanding of the basic concepts and principles of intellectual property and their application in the specifics of concrete users of traditional knowledge. There are many inherent problems in applying these concepts to real life situations. For example, for patenting, it is essential that the inventions reflect and element of novelty, Non-obviousness and industrial usefulness, which may not hold true in case of most of the traditional knowledge perse.

Many initiatives have been taken to consider the protection of traditional knowledge base from the legal angle. The thrust of most initiatives is to develop a system that documents and preserves traditional knowledge created in the past, and contributes to the promotion and dissemination of innovations. Such a system might provide appropriate information for continuing creativity and innovation in most fields of technology including traditional, medicinal and agricultural practices. An important step is to establish digital databases to enable quick retrieval of information of traditional knowledge for a variety of uses.

UPOV SYSTEM

A sue generis system was created for protection of new varieties of plants by International convention for protection of new varieties of plants (UPOV) in 1961 on realization that the conditions of patentability might not be appropriate for the plant varieties. Subsequently, the Act was modified in the 1978 and then in 1991. Basic purpose of UPOV is to ensure national treatment for any breeder of the world at par with domestic breeders. The UPOV 1991 made the breeders rights more precise. While TRIPS (Trade Related Aspects of Intellectual Property Rights agreement) does not explicity state that sui generis system should be compatible with provisions of International Union of Plant Variety (UPOV), it is implied that such should be the case. India is not a member of UPOV.

IPR ISSUES

Some of the key issues relating to the protection intellectual property rights are indicated below.

- Life Forms – plants, animals and micro-organisms
- Genetically Modified Organisms (GMO)
- Medicinal Plants and Herbs
- Traditional Knowledge
- Biodiversity
- Internet (Domain names, web publishing)
- Software
- Databases
- Others

Plant related patents

There are a large number of examples where in plant –based inventions have been patented across the world. Patenting activity has been observed, for example, inventions pertaining to the medicinal plants, spices, fruits, vegetables, wood, dyes, and fibber. In medicinal plants, patents have been granted for inventions relating to Nicotiana tabacum, Azadirachta indica Aloe vera, Croton tiglium and Cannabis sativa. In plants like Withania somnifera Picrorhiza kurroa, Achyranthes aspera, and Commiphora mukul, the patenting has rather been limited. In spices, patents were obtained for inventions relating to Cinnamomum camphora, Cinnamomum zeylanicum, Mentha spicata, and Zingiber officinale. In fruits, patenting activity was observed in case of Musa paradisiaca, Tamarindus indica, and Mangifera indica. In vegetables, Citrus limon, Allium sativum, Daucus carota, and Cucumis melo received attention. Boswella serrata was one of the active plants in the category of wood. Indigofera tinctoria and Lawsonia inermis were found to be given attention by the inventors in patenting. High level of patenting activity was related to the plants, namely Cocos nucifera and Linum usitatissimum in the fiber category.

Management of IPRs

Management of IPRs has one connotation to and individual inventor with limited financial resources at one end of the spectrum, a different connotation for organised R&D institutions like national R&D laboratories and quite another to giant multinational corporations on the other end. To some the management of IPRs covers merely the period from the original research through the grants of patents while to some others it means the process of management after the signing of a license contract leading to transfer of technology and commercialization. In abroad sense, the concept of the management of IPRs covers the administration of all phases of management from the original concept of the invention to the final commercialization of the invention.

There are many aspects, which need to be effectively addressed by R&D organizations in this context. Some of these are identified as follows:

- An early assessment of the commercial potential of the research being undertaken.
- Awareness of the scientists and mangers of R&D on the protection of intellectual property.
- Determining means of protecting the invention e.g. through patents or under plant variety protection.
- How the product involved is to be marketed by the inventor?
- Establishment of a good system of keeping records from the stage of first conception of the idea to an account of all activities carried out through various stages of the progress of R&D project.
- Keeping track of the trends, the developments in patent literature in the field in which research is being undertaken.

- Management of contractual relationships between employers and employee with regard to ownership of invention, sharing of the benefits and keeping confidentiality of the Know-how and other technical information.
- Management of IPR related aspects during joint R&D collaborations between R&D institutions and industrial firms as well as collaboration with similar organizations under international cooperation programmes.
- Coordination between R&D, Marketing, Legal and other technical units/functions for protection of IPRs.
- Managing the process of licensing of the patent and transfer of technology

Knowledge intensive agriculture

Research and technology are the cornerstones of sustainable agriculture and rural development. There are greater opportunities for interactions among countries to share information and experiences in linking national goals, research capabilities and farmers' needs. Building partnerships emphasis on pre-breeding programs in crop improvement, enhancement of genetic resources, biotechnology research in the field of molecular biology, especially the transgenics, basic and strategic work in natural resource conservation, are likely to be useful.

The agricultural research in India has made significant developments. For example in rice, India is amongst the leading countries to develop commercially viable rice hybrids, for example, its dwarf varieties including Pusa Basmati 1; Jaya, the high yielding variety for irrigated areas, Vikramaraya, the rice –tungro virus resistant variety; Ajaya, a bacterial blight resistant variety and Suraksha – a multiple resistant variety. In maize, a number of hybrids and composites suitable for different climatic conditions and product requirements have been developed and yield increased. In wheat, more than 200 varieties have been developed for irrigated and rain fed conditions in different parts of the country and for different sowing timings including varieties resistant against wheat diseases. In oil seeds too a number of new developments have led to self-sufficiency. Major research efforts have also been taken for development of hybrid seeds in vegetables, fruits, horticulture, potato production, and application of tissue culture in banana. In livestock sector, production of cross breeds of cattle and their wide adoption has greatly contributed to country's milk production. Embryo transfer technology is being used to improve the productivity in cattle, buffalo, sheep and goats. New technologies in fisheries have led to credible increase in prawn farming.

These developments indicate all round capabilities for the knowledge-based innovations in the agricultural system. The knowledge intensity of agricultural research is likely to grow in the future. The intellectual property rights are likely to play an important role. The awareness in IPR and their management by the R&D institutions and scientists is and essential pre-requisite in exploiting these capabilities for commercial and societal gains.

References

1 Pushpangadan P and Narayanan Nair K, Future of systematic and biodiversity research in India: need for a national consortium and national agenda for systematic biology research, Current secence, 80 (5) 2001,631-638.

2 Gupta V. K., Negotiating IPR in International Science and Technology cooperation,"Journal of Intellectual Property Rights, 5 (March 2000) 61-71.

3 Karki, MMS and Gupta V.K. Natural Product Innovations: Taxol, Journal of Intellectual Property Rights, 5 (July 2000)206-210.

4 Gupta V. K., Protecting confidential R&D information, Tech Monitor Jouunal of Asian pacific centre for transfer of technology, 17 (3) (May-June 1999) 37-42.

5 Prajneshu Meenakshi and Gupta, V. K., Traditional Knowledge Database: IPR and Opportunities for R&D, Journal of Intellectual Property Rights,November 2001.

6 Prajneshu Meenakshi and Gupta, V.K., Patenting in Clove accepted for publication in the journal of Intellectual Property Rights.